Kiss the Sky

Kiss the Sky

My Weekend in Monterey
at the Greatest Concert Ever

by **Dusty Baker**

FIRST EDITION
ISBN 978-0-9854-1908-0

Wellstone Books
an imprint of the Wellstone Center in the Redwoods
858 Amigo Road
Soquel, CA 95073

Distributed by Publishers Group West

Contents

Chapter 1
Music Made Me

I t's almost like I can't even function without music. I need it around me at all times, and it's always been there for me, morning, afternoon and night, from the time I was a boy. Music makes me who I am. Music helps put me in the mood I want to be in. When I'm angry, I listen to certain music. When I want to be mellow, I listen to other music. When I'm in a hurry to be somewhere, then I drive along in my truck or car listening to music that I *move* to. When I just want to chill out and feel relaxed and happy, then I listen to reggae, which is probably why reggae is my favorite. I love jazz. I love the blues. I love rock. Sometimes I'll put on classical. I even listen to country music now and then because really it's just the other side of the blues when you think about it. But reggae is the music I turn to most often. To me the more music you know, the more artists you've heard, the more styles you've explored, the more insight you have into how all kinds of different people think and feel. In other words, to me music is not only something I love, not only something I enjoy, music is something I believe can help anyone become a well-rounded individual — deeper, more open and more aware.

Music was always around us growing up in Riverside, California. My mom's main guy was Lou Rawls. Every morning, we knew it was time to get up out of bed when we heard "Tobacco Road." I got so tired of hearing that song! She loved a good melody and wanted music that she could sing along to like Johnny Mathis or anything out of Motown. She liked a big, booming, soulful voice, someone like Mahalia Jackson. My mama, she *loved* Mahalia Jackson. My mom sang in the choir at the Park Avenue Baptist Church and made us sing, too. That was the established African-American church, traditional and old school. The Park Avenue Baptist Church was right across the street from a pool hall, and I knew I better not *dare* be caught coming out of that pool hall. No! Everybody in town would tell on you. Everybody in town would reprimand you and take you home to your parents and then you got reprimanded again. Consequently, very few of us got into any kind of trouble. That was the epitome of a village raising a child.

My mom used to forbid us to hang around at the Pentecostal church, because they were the first church that had drums and guitars, and you could go to the Pentecostal church and pick up some dance moves. Everybody got happy and stuff, you know what I mean? I'd be looking through the window of the Pentecostal church to check out some of those dance moves, along with my friend Ray Salcedo, without my mom knowing. Now Ray is a Pentecostal minister.

My dad was the straightest man in the world, but he was into Miles Davis. That was his guy. I didn't understand Miles. I really didn't. But I *liked* Miles and I picked up an attraction to Miles and to jazz from my dad. He was also into the blues, that was his favorite, and you knew he was home from working his two or three jobs when blues started filling up the house. I didn't understand the message of the blues, but I liked the melody of it and the rhythmic sounds that the blues had. I didn't know they were singing about oppression. I could tell something was wrong, I just didn't know *what* was wrong. My dad was always listening to the blues and a lot of his friends were musicians.

My mother had me taking piano lessons. That was not my first choice, believe me. I was always infatuated with the guitar and wanted to learn to play, but my mother said no way. I also loved the saxophone, so in eighth grade I signed up for a music course at school and the teacher told me no. She said I could not play the sax because I had the wrong lips. What was she talking about? Wrong lips? I went home that night and stared at myself in the mirror, trying to figure it out. "Man, what's wrong with my lips?" I was wondering. "They ain't too big and they're not too skinny. I see people playing sax with all kinds of lips. And that teacher told me I had the wrong lips?"

My mother tried hard to give her five kids some culture, starting with me as the oldest. She was always looking for ways to help us be respectable. She ran a charm school for black girls in Riverside, because she'd tried to do some modeling and had the experience of being accepted on a job over the phone only to show up in person and find out that as an African-American she would not even be considered.

To this day I still run into women who my mama taught at that charm school.

I remember once when she made us take dancing lessons and I had to learn how to do the foxtrot. I wanted so much to ask her: Why are you making us do this when you never dance like this yourself? Sometimes my parents would host parties and I tell you when it came to it they could get down, if you know what I'm saying. They could jitterbug like nobody's business. But of course I didn't dare talk back to my mother like that. My father would never have allowed that. He was big and strong, built like the running back Jim Brown, and you did not want to see him get angry. Mama would make us go to classical concerts, and the funny thing was, she thought I loved those classical concerts, because I'd be smiling and nodding my head, but that was just because I kept a transistor radio in my pocket and would listen to Dodgers games during the concert whenever I could. I actually hated those concerts. I'd have rather been listening to James Brown.

My mother pushed me to take piano lessons because she thought that would be a good grounding in music for me. She saw piano as the basis for all music. She figured I could always get around to taking guitar later on, but I never got to later on. She made me play piano recitals in front of our church and I'll never forget that. I had to bow and all my buddies were there, snickering as I banged my way through the "Hungarian Rhapsody No. 2," followed by the "Blue Danube." I was so embarrassed, man.

I figured if I was going to learn the piano, I'd learn to play like Little Richard. I didn't understand a man wearing makeup, that was kind of confusing to me, but he was cool and he made that piano rock. Then I heard Jerry Lee Lewis playing on *The Ed Sullivan Show* one Sunday night and I loved everything about that cat's style. He was the one I was going to emulate. One day my mother came home and I had my feet up on top of the piano and was pounding away. When my mother saw that she had a fit.

"Have you lost your mind?" were the first words out of her mouth.

What was I going to say to that? I stared back at her.

"Get your feet off that piano!" she yelled.

"Mama! Jerry Lee Lewis!"

"You're Dusty Baker! You're no Jerry Lee Lewis!"

No one in my family ever called me anything but "Dusty." My mother gave me that name because even when I was a toddler I was always getting into something and looked like I'd been rolling around in the dirt half the time, like the character from *Peanuts*. No one was going to call me "John," my given name. There was one John in the house, my father, Johnnie B. Baker Sr., and there wasn't room for another John. My dad was a commanding figure. Everyone respected him. I didn't see him get mad at me very many times — not unless I'd really earned it — but I'll never forget those occasions. Like the time I stole a Mr. Goodbar chocolate bar from Mr. Carlos' store in Riverside. Oh you should have seen my father! Another time, he found out I'd been hiding dice under my pillow. He took them, walked out to the driveway — and used a hammer to pound them into dust! Those lessons stayed with me. All of us, but especially me as the oldest of five, had it deeply instilled in us to be responsible and to remember the difference between right and wrong.

My dad grew up in Lakeland, Florida, which might be why he always liked to fish and passed that love on to me. My mother was born in Indio, California, out in the desert past Palm Springs, and her parents had moved there from Oklahoma to pick dates. In World War II my dad served in the Navy, stationed on a destroyer patrolling the Pacific, and later talked about seeing Japanese kamikaze pilots plunging into the ocean. After the war he took a civilian job at Norton Air Force Base in San Bernardino, not far from Riverside, which was where my parents met and where they got married. My dad didn't want to live in Florida, because in those years the only work that would have been available to him there was picking fruit. He wanted to make a better life for himself.

That's why he always worked at least two jobs the whole time I was growing up. For thirty-six years my father worked at least two jobs at a time. His main job was working for the military as a civilian, but if you ask me what he did I couldn't tell you, because to this day I don't know. He kept that secret. For all I know he was some kind of spy. One time when I was old enough to drive, I remember it was summertime, and I'd dropped him off at the base, so I knew where his building was, and I had his car. He'd told me never to visit him at work. His words were: *Don't ever come in here.* And when my father told you something, you listened. But I was always wondering what he actually did. So one day I got bold. I showed up at the base and found the building where he worked. I was peeking over a partition and a military cop came up and grabbed me and in no time had me up against the wall. I was trying to tell him I was just there to visit my father, but the MP wasn't listening to anything I said. My dad heard my voice and came out, and once I saw the look on his face, I'd have rather it was just the MP and me! He was hot!

"I told you never to come in here!" he told me.

I never went back, and he never told me what he did for the military, which was kind of strange since he and I spent so much time together. I was the oldest, so usually when he went out on one of his second jobs, I'd go with him. We might drive around selling eggs from the hens in our back yard, along with bacon, and don't even ask me where my dad got his hands on bacon, or we'd tack seats at the movie theater or do janitorial work. We'd do gardening jobs wherever we could find them. I remember going right across the bridge to the houses where people with more money lived and we'd mow lawns there. Often kids I went to school with lived in those houses and I'd see them at school. I'll never forget mowing the lawn of one kid in my school whose house was the biggest one in town. It was so big it had an elevator, and from that day on I always told my friends that one day I was going to have a house with my own elevator. Now I've got an elevator in my home, all because of that kid whose lawns we cut back in Riverside.

It was a good place to grow up, Riverside, about an hour east of Los Angeles, known to most people if it was known at all as a stop on the road to Palm Springs or for the oranges that grew around there or for the Mission Inn, the kind of place presidents stayed. Teddy Roosevelt and William Howard Taft stayed there. Herbert Hoover stayed there. John F. Kennedy stayed there. Tricky Dick Nixon was married there and Ronald and Nancy Reagan were there on their honeymoon. It was a fancy place, considered the largest structure built in what's called a Mission Revival style, though really the place is a hodgepodge of architectural styles, but they pull it off real well. It was a place for presidents to stay but not, my whole time growing up in Riverside, a place for black people. We couldn't even set foot there. Nowadays if I'm visiting Southern California, I love to stay in the Mission Inn. I was just there recently, in fact, and it was beautiful. I felt right at home. It's especially nice if you go down around Christmastime and they have the place decked out with lights and all the decorations.

In the '50s when I was a boy in Riverside it grew from less than 50,000 people to more than 84,000, and it would grow a lot more than that later, but back then it was a country town. I grew up in a community that was about half white, about a quarter Mexican and about a quarter black. I'm not guessing at those numbers. That's how it was. I look at grade school pictures of myself and count the students one by one and, sure enough, about half white, with Mexicans and blacks making up the rest in about the same numbers. It was the same on my Little League teams.

The other thing I notice about those Little League pictures is my dad, always there in the back row, like when I was eleven and played for the Bridgeport Brass Rockets. He was the coach. I stand there now staring at my dad in those pictures, coaching a bunch of kids, and sometimes if I stare long enough I have the feeling I'm seeing him for the first time. As kids even if we're bright and curious and open-eyed, we're still half-blind most of the time when it comes

to seeing our parents. My dad was just my dad.
I knew he was proud and strong and determined.
I knew he had an iron will. I also knew he loved life
and loved us. But as a kid, you can't begin to put
into perspective all your parents do for you. Here
my dad was, working at least two jobs all the time,
and he always found time to be there to coach us,
and to do so much for us that we didn't even fully
grasp at the time. He'd come home from one job and
take a twenty-minute nap and then go to the other,
that's how busy he was, but all those years he never
missed one of my games.

When I go back to Riverside now and talk to people, they all want to tell me about my dad and how
much respect he had. He was respected by blacks.
He was respected in the Mexican community. He
was respected by everyone. He was the man. Every
season, we'd need uniforms and equipment for
Little League, and every season he'd somehow come
through and get all of that donated. I don't know
how he did it, but we always had equipment for
everybody. He could sell anybody on anything and
he'd always win over some sponsors to take care of
all that.

When you're Little League age, the important

thing is not to have someone trying to be a *great* coach who will insist on drilling every last subtlety of the game into you. You're a kid! What you need is a *good* coach, who can be patient and understanding, someone who can ground kids in the fundamentals but also keep it enjoyable. My dad was that coach. "An important lesson that I hope they learn is to be patient and understand and think about other people and how they feel," he used to say. "Don't be too quick to criticize."

After the games, depending on how we did, we'd get free A&W root beer along with a burger, and that always got us going. We were playing for the root beer! How many Little League coaches can say they coached two future big leaguers? Not that many, but my dad helped mold both myself and Bobby Bonds into ballplayers. Bobby was three years older than me and one of the best athletes I've seen in my whole life. He was definitely the best athlete to come out of the Riverside area. Later he'd become the first big-league player to hit thirty home runs and steal thirty bases in three different seasons. Bobby was strong and he could flat-out run.

Our families were tight. In fact, Bobby's older sister, Rosie, used to babysit me. She was a great athlete as well, and ran the hurdles for the U.S. in the 1964 Tokyo Olympics. Ten years before that she used to look after me. Later she told the story of how my father paid her five dollars to babysit me, and somehow I found a way to sneak off and was walking down the street. She tracked me down. I was all of five years old then.

"Dusty, what are you doing?" she called down to me. "You're costing me five dollars!"

Bobby Bonds was like a big brother to me. I wanted to be just like him. He played football, basketball and baseball and ran track, so I played football, basketball and baseball and ran track. He competed in the long jump wearing his baseball uniform, since he had no time to change, so I later competed in the long jump wearing my baseball uniform. When I was a kid I went everywhere with Bobby, so long as he let me, which was most of the time. Sometimes he would let me play with him and the other older guys, where normally they wouldn't let any of the younger kids play. Just watching those guys in action was great for my development, they were so talented, but getting to compete against Bobby and the others was even better. You learn fast when everyone is far more skilled than you are.

Bobby married young and by July '64 he was a father. I held that baby boy in my arms shortly after he was born, young Barry Lamar Bonds.

Chapter 2

My Eighteenth Birthday Present From My Mom

My Mom couldn't stand James Brown. She said he didn't sing, he just shouted. But the lyrics and the larger message James Brown was delivering were necessary at that point in our history. He was saying: I'm black and I'm proud. He was saying that before the Black Power movement of the 1960s — you know, those two San Jose State sprinters raising their clenched fists during the National Anthem at the 1968 Mexico City Olympics — and James was delivering that message in a way that might have been easier for some to take. That was a major occurrence back in the day. Music had a message but it didn't have the baggage of so much else. Like if you were listening to Gil Scott-Heron, who was basically a rap artist before there was rap, or if you were listening to the Doors,

Jim Morrison doing his whole Lizard King thing, it didn't matter if those dudes were white or black or green. What mattered was that they were cool and you could identify with them, especially at that point in time. People would say to me, "That's white music" or "That's black music." I didn't know what they were talking about. Not really. To me music really don't have any color to it.

That was one reason I was intrigued, when I was growing up, by what I heard about England and the English sound. The people over there were into music and they didn't care about color the way so many Americans did, or at least not when it came to U.S. artists, especially not U.S. jazz artists. Billie Holiday, Dinah Washington, Lena Horne, Eartha Kitt — all those great singers my mama loved so much, they were accepted and honored in England and France and all over Europe. That was the beauty of it. Music forced people to cross cultures.

Take a guy I knew growing up in Riverside, Rod Piazza. He was a couple years older than me, a white guy who loved the blues. He was always buying new blues records and listening to those and wanting to talk about it. He knew I was into that music, too, so he'd ask me what I thought of Junior Wells or

Sonny Boy Williamson. Rod had tried to play guitar when he was just a little kid, but apparently his older brother took him to a Jimmy Reed concert one time and they went backstage and talked to Jimmy Reed. Jimmy told Rod that he was better off playing harmonica than guitar and even gave him one to start practicing. So all I remember of Rod is that he always had that harmonica and he'd be doing his best to make it purr, but he had a long way to go. "Shut up, man!" we'd tell poor Rod. "You making all that noise!" He ignored us and kept practicing — and practicing and practicing. Before long he had his own band and was opening for Howlin' Wolf! Can you believe it? Later I saw him at Sweetwater in Mill Valley, one of my favorite places to see music in the Bay Area, right up there with Slim's in the city.

When I was fourteen years old, my father's job at Norton Air Force Base was discontinued. He was given a choice: He could take a new job and move us to Ogden, Utah, or Sacramento, California. That was not a choice he had to ponder long. So he went to work at McClellan Air Force Base in Northern California, twenty minutes northeast of Sacramento. My dad found a real-estate agent to look for a new house, and the agent only wanted to show him houses in black neighborhoods — so my dad went off on his own and found a house he liked in the nearby community of Carmichael, which was only a mile and a half from Del Campo High School. I went from living in a mixed community to being one of only two blacks at the whole school, the other one being my little brother Robert.

One thing about sports is it always helps you make new friends, especially if you're one of the stars, and I made some good friends at Del Campo through sports, like Brad Johnson and Dennis Kludt, who turned into lifelong friends. We were all into music and the thing was, growing up in Riverside I'd had a great grounding in all kinds of music, from Billie Holiday and Lou Rawls to the blues, the music that inspired artists like the Rolling Stones and the Doors and a lot of the best new music. Now I was making friends who pointed me in new directions and I was hearing all kinds of new stuff that hadn't been on my radar before. I was checking out the Mamas & the Papas with Big Mama Cass singing "California Dreamin'." I was tuning into Eric Burdon and the Animals and Buffalo Springfield and Big Brother and the Holding Company, with Janis Joplin singing. I was listening to singer-songwriters like Bob Dylan and Van Morrison and digging how deep they were.

I've always liked good writing. My mama had all kinds of deep books in our house when I was growing up, black writers and thinkers like Eldridge Cleaver, Langston Hughes, James Baldwin, W.E.B. DuBois, Frederick Douglass and Marcus Garvey. She also liked Malcolm X and Martin Luther King Jr., and wanted us to know that we could like both of them, understand both of them, and not have that be a contradiction. She knew we weren't going to study every one of those books she had in the house, but she insisted we take a look and have an idea what each was about and what that writer had to say. She told us we had to be better to get any-where in life, whether it be in sports or in academics or you name it. Later I'd even study journalism at college because I thought I wanted to be a writer. I remember when I first discovered Dylan and Van Morrison. I loved the message. Most people hear the drums, the guitar, the keyboard, but they don't listen to the lyrics and the message. I've always tuned into the message.

Everyone was excited about music, there was so much going on in San Francisco and the Bay Area.

Before long my friends and I began talking about forming our own garage band, even if we weren't any good and had only practiced a few times. Guess who they wanted for their singer? I was going to sing "The House of the Rising Sun," because we wanted to sound like Eric Burdon and the Animals, who did that song. I'd be the only black dude in the group. I was going to be Hootie and the Blowfish before Hootie. My dad put his foot down. He said I already had enough on my plate getting my homework done and playing four sports at Del Campo and I wasn't going to be messing around in a garage band trying to sing with so much else for me to do. End of discussion.

My parents were our anchors. They were both such strong people in their own way. My dad was all about discipline and duty, devoted to family above all else. My mother was just as devoted to family, but she was also more tuned into the times. She was interested in the spirit of rebellion in the air and she herself was a little bit of a rebel in her own way. During my senior year at Del Campo she and my dad got into some kind of big argument that my brothers and sisters and I never understood, not even me as the oldest. It seemed to build up and build up some more. Then one day we got the news that my parents were splitting up and my father was moving out. He found an apartment for himself near American River College. My dad's discipline had sometimes been hard on me, but I loved him and I needed him and now he wasn't living with us anymore. I was the man of the house. I was the one who had to make sure the lawn was mowed and clean up after the dog every day and everything else, too. I was in shock.

I'd been having a good basketball season at Del Campo. The team had improved from the year before when we missed so many shots, I got a workout on the boards. Now in my senior year we were playing well. I was averaging more than twenty points a game and, early in the season, having a great time. I *loved* basketball. I've always thought of it as my favorite sport. Cheech and Chong used to do a whole thing about "Basketball Jones" in a real high-pitched voice. (*Basketball Jones, I got a basketball Jones....*) Well, that was me, I was Basketball Jones, except I didn't sleep with the ball. But after my parents split and we heard the word "divorce" for the first time, I didn't know which way was which. I could still play, but I was a mess at practice. I was usually a pretty easy-going guy before that, given to joking around, but suddenly I was withdrawn from the others and even irritable sometimes. I was also missing shots I'd normally make.

My coach, Eli McCullough, finally told me we had to talk. Coach McCullough knew basketball but he also knew people, and he could tell something was not right. He cared about me. He hoped he could help me — not because he wanted to win, although that was important, too, but because he liked me and saw I was going through a lot.

"You were always an upbeat guy and then you were very quiet and moody in practice," Coach McCullough said when I called him up to check his recollections of that time.

So we talked. I told him about my parents. And he listened. More than anything, he listened. We had a series of talks like that. Practice was at night, not ending until nine o'clock, and sometimes we'd sit there in the gym afterward talking until midnight. I was the oldest of five, and saw everything that happened with my family as my responsibility.

"I finally convinced you that the divorce was not your fault and that now it was your job to support both your parents and your brothers and sisters," Coach McCullough recalls.

I took that advice to heart. One thing it meant to me was that I was going to have a harder time making a decision on whether to play professional baseball or go to college on a scholarship for football, basketball or baseball and maybe track, too. It started with simple math: Our family never had extra money. We had what we needed. We had a good life. But it took a lot of hard work from my parents. Now my father was living in his own apartment and had to pay monthly rent. As a family we had less money than we had before. I was the oldest of five, and it was very important in our house growing up that everyone have the opportunity to go to college. I was all-city in baseball and all-county in basketball, football and track. The recruiters were after me. If I took a scholarship, I'd get to be big man on campus. I'd have a great time, I was sure, but I wouldn't be helping my family any. I'd just be helping myself. If I had a chance to play pro ball, the money I made could help support my brothers and sisters. I could help pay for their educations.

Of all the recruiters who came my way, Carroll Williams of Santa Clara University stood out. He was assistant coach then, heading up recruitment efforts, but would serve as head basketball coach from 1970 to 1992. He'd been a good player at San

Jose State and he and I connected. Even so, I was careful about the recruiters. I remember once when Coach McCullough told me that three recruiters were waiting for me after one of our Del Campo basketball games, I let him know what my priorities were.

"Coach," I told him, "I don't want to talk to any recruiters during the season. My focus is on the team and winning."

Coach Williams was in regular contact and finally after basketball season I agreed to come to Santa Clara for a campus visit that May. I should tell you that Santa Clara did have one big thing going for it: That was where my dad wanted me to go. He figured a private Jesuit university like that would be a great place for me to get a good education and not get too wild. I was more intrigued by San Jose State and Arizona State. I was over at a buddy's house and noticed a *Playboy* magazine belonging to his father. I flipped through that — what teenage boy would not flip through a *Playboy*? — and there was an article on the biggest party schools in the country. That got my attention. Right there at the top of the list, in black and white: San Jose State and Arizona State. That didn't sound too bad to me! I told my father what I was thinking and he was as against that as he was against me singing "House of the Rising Sun" in a garage band.

"San Jose State and Arizona State are the top two party schools in the country!" he told me.

Wait a minute? Had my dad been reading *Playboy*? Where else had he picked up that piece of information? I wanted to ask him — oh how I wanted to ask him — if he'd been reading *Playboy*, but it would have been a very, very bad idea for me to open my mouth.

Coach Williams had driven to the Sacramento area to see me many times, and he picked me up and took me back for that May 1967 campus visit. I didn't have a car, so that was really the only option. We both liked to hunt and fish, so we would always talk about that.

"I had to drive up after a game and it was late at night as we were driving back," Coach Williams recalls. "In Hercules, with all the oil refineries, we hit a deer that had crossed the freeway. I saw it at the last second and it hit the side of the bumper. We both got out of the car to take a look and saw that the deer was dead. We were both shaken up by that. We had a good relationship because we both loved to fish. We talked about a lot of places to fish in the Sierra."

I was down in Santa Clara for the weekend, and they put me in the dorms with some of the guys on the basketball team. Terry O'Brien, a Broncos guard, hosted me and kind of introduced me around and kept an eye on me. I met the Ogden brothers, who would combine to average 27.9 points that season for a good Santa Clara team that made it all the way to the NCAA West Regional Final, where it lost to Lew Alcindor and the UCLA team that would win the title that year. I also met a bunch of baseball players, like big Bob Spence, who the White Sox would take in the first round that year, and Albert and Alvin Strane, the only two black guys on the team, who played shortstop and second base. They were from Oakland and showed me around.

The highlight of the visit for me came that Sunday and was completely unexpected. There was a benefit concert taking place at Mission Garden on the Santa Clara University campus, starting at one o'clock, and the lineup was Vince Guaraldi, Cal Tjader and the Jefferson Airplane. I was definitely into checking *that* out! What a day it was out there, too, a beautiful warm Northern California day, sunny and full of promise.

Here's the account of that concert published in

the *Redwoods*, a Santa Clara student publication: "Santa Clara's first Spring Festival was a day of high temperatures, high spirits, and high minds," reads the article. "Al Collins, well known KSFO disc jockey, functioned as emcee wearing his new seersucker 'jump suit.' ... While Cal Tjader and Vince Guaraldi were well received, the Airplane really generated a festival attitude among the audience seated before them. Many in the audience began dancing on the grass, others merely ran and jumped around like 'Flower Children,' and all this occurred under the shadow of a giant banana poster, anonymously hung from a window of Montgomery Hall."

*   *   *

I'd been so careful about not letting the recruiters get to me during basketball season, but I didn't do as well during baseball season that year. A lot of big-league ball clubs were scouting me and I let it throw me off. I was trying to impress the scouts. They'd say, "How far can you hit a ball?" And I'd go out there and swing for the fences and strike out. That wasn't my game. I never struck out. I was so messed up, I was almost down near the Mendoza Line at times during my senior year.

Going into the Major League Baseball amateur player draft in June 1967, my mentality was that I was as good as anyone out there and ought to be taken somewhere in the first round. Maybe not in the top five, but somewhere in the round. I do remember thinking: "Please, let it be anyone but the Atlanta Braves that drafts me!" I did not want to go live in the South. I'd been dealing with enough racism in Northern California and I was sure Georgia would be much worse. So when the Braves, choosing twelfth overall, selected a guy named Andrew Finlay, I had mixed feelings. Finlay was an outfielder for Luther Burbank High in Sacramento and I'd played against him. I knew he was good, but I didn't think he was any better than me. I didn't want to be drafted by the Braves, but I did want someone to take me in the first round. No such luck. Nor was I chosen in the second round — or the third or the fourth or the fifth. Or the tenth or twentieth. Would you believe it? I was not chosen until the twenty-sixth round! I was taken 503rd overall! You want to tell me there were five HUNDRED other guys more talented than me? I don't think so. And which team drafted me? The Atlanta Braves.

Good thing I had a birthday that month. On June

15 I turned eighteen years old and my mother gave me one of the great presents a mother could ever give a son: two tickets to the three-day Monterey Pop Festival that weekend, along with twenty bucks and use of the family car. I almost couldn't believe it. This was beyond my craziest dreams. I'd been cutting out now and then to catch concerts in Berkeley or San Francisco, but those were single events. This was going to be three full days of music, thousands of young people all feeling good, looking good, ready to enjoy themselves, and not only was I going, I could bring a friend — my buddy Dennis couldn't come, so I asked my good friend Gary Woodrell and he couldn't believe his good luck. This was going to be epic! John Phillips of the Mamas & the Papas was one of the lead organizers of the ambitious event, really the first true rock-and-roll festival. Two years later the organizers of another major rock event in Woodstock, New York, would use Monterey as their template. For me as an eighteen-year-old kid, this was like being invited to the best party ever, where I'd get a chance to see all the bands I'd been wanting to see and a bunch of bands I didn't even know I needed to see.

Chapter 3
Feelin' Groovy

'm not kidding when I tell you that for Gary and me, the highlight of the whole weekend might have been that feeling we had getting into my mom's white AMC Rambler Classic station wagon and driving out of Sacramento knowing we were on our way to the adventure of our lives. It was a feeling of pure freedom. In those years I was always needing to be here or needing to be there. My mom ran a tight ship and as the oldest, I had a lot of responsibilities. That weekend I had none. Gary and I couldn't stop grinning at each other as we set out from Carmichael, just east of Sacramento, and especially as we drove up over the bridge taking us across the wide, flat Sacramento River, California's largest. We crossed over that river and it hit home that we were escaping the dense, dry

ninety-five-degree heat of Sacramento in summer for a different kind of heat down on the foggy
Monterey Peninsula.

For us driving west always brought a thrill.
This was before anyone started talking about the
Summer of Love. The Monterey Pop Festival would
launch the Summer of Love. Word would spread of
what went down there and it would bring young
people to San Francisco from all over the country,
maybe all over the world. You might have heard a
famous song from that period — I'd sing it for you,
but that takes hitting some high notes — "If you're
going to San Francisco/ Be sure to wear some flow-
ers in your hair." If you're anywhere near my age,
you could recite the song in your sleep. If you're
younger, take a minute to cue it up online, because
it captures the feeling of that summer perfectly.
In fact, it was released just a few weeks before
Gary and I climbed into my mom's Rambler for the
drive to Monterey and it was sitting at No. 4 on the
Billboard Hot 100 chart the weekend of the festival.
It was written by John Phillips of the Mamas & the
Papas (I'd caught them in Berkeley or S.F. already
at that point), produced along with Lou Adler, and
sung by Scott MacKenzie, and it was specifically

released to promote the festival Gary and I were on our way to attending. That song was like a promise of everything to come, if only you were cool enough to take part. Gary and I were cool enough — well, I was, anyway (just kidding, Gary).

When the song talked about "San Francisco," it didn't so much mean a peninsula of land just south of the Golden Gate Bridge, although that was the center of the action; it was talking about a feeling. Gary and I might as well have had that song ringing in our ears along that whole drive. I'm sure it came on the radio that day.

All across the nation
Such a strange vibration
People in motion
There's a whole generation
With a new explanation
People in motion
People in motion

We were in motion! Damn, were we in motion! We liked the part about how there was going to be a "love-in" that summer in the streets of San Francisco. You kidding me? We were two eighteen-year-old kids. We were driving down to Monterey to catch the music, but we were also looking forward to a smorgasbord of beautiful girls, all dressed up to look good and all in great moods. You could get high just walking past a group of girls like that and taking a deep breath.

There's a scene in the movie *The Graduate*, which came out that year, where the young guy played by Dustin Hoffman is cruising along in his little red convertible, a 1966 Alfa Romeo, driving toward the church where Elaine is getting married, jamming to the strumming guitar of Simon and Garfunkel's "Mrs. Robinson," when all of a sudden the music starts sputtering and you get it right away — the dude is running out of gas. Even though he'd just stopped at a gas station to make a payphone call! It was kind of like that for Gary and me that day on the way to Monterey. We drove in from the heat of Sacramento, past the Nut Tree in the Vacaville area, through Fairfield and Vallejo, and finally turned the corner past Richmond and were driving along the East Bay toward Berkeley, with the pale-blue waters of San Francisco Bay spreading out toward the San Francisco skyline and Golden Gate Bridge in the distance. Every time you saw that view, it gave you the feeling in the pit of your stomach that you were just where you wanted to be.

THWUMP!

Gary and I didn't hear any guitar strumming that told us we were running out of gas, we heard a sudden thwump that told us we had a flat tire. Oh no! Neither of us was much when it came to fixing cars. Dennis was the car guy in our group. We pulled over to the side of the road and got out of the Rambler. Only then did we notice that all four tires on my mom's car were totally bald. We hauled the jack out of the trunk and went to work. We were cursing and laughing and wondering if we'd ever get the car going again. Somehow we did. We got the spare on there, which meant we now had three bald tires and a spare — and we had another two hours down to Monterey, and a three-and-a-half-hour drive back on Sunday. Twice we'd have to drive the twisty mountain road through the Santa Cruz Mountains, Highway 17. But no way were we turning back. We had too much waiting for us up ahead in Monterey.

Back in Sacramento it had been hot, but the closer we got to Monterey, the cooler it felt. We didn't care about that. By the time we drove past Moss Landing, spitting distance from the Monterey Fairgrounds, I was feeling like a sprinter on the blocks, ready to get out and burn off some energy. As we were getting close, the concert had already started and my mother's favorite, Lou Rawls, was singing to the kids gathered in Monterey. He even sang "Tobacco Road," the song I'd woken up to so many mornings.

I'm not going to say I remember every detail for sure almost half a century later — forty-eight years as I write these words — but we parked and made our way in during Johnny Rivers' set and the first song I can clearly remember hearing was "Baby I Need Your Loving," that great Motown tune, written and recorded by the Four Tops in 1964, that Rivers had covered that year. Rivers was best known for doing the song for a spy show on TV over in England, *Secret Agent Man*. That was the song he sang to close his set and next up was Eric Burdon and the Animals, who had inspired me to want to be in a garage band. They started off with a tune called "San Francisco Nights," and Burdon was singing about a "warm San Francisco night," an idea that would seem pretty funny to anyone who ever spent a night at Candlestick Park. I later found out Burdon wrote the song after hanging out in S.F. with Janis Joplin during a heat spell, but I didn't know that then and had no idea what he was talking about singing "Old child young child feel all right/ On a warm San Francisco night," but I guess it makes sense now. The Animals closed with a very trippy version of "Paint It Black" by the Rolling Stones, who we all hoped would be in Monterey, but both Mick Jagger and Keith Richard had recently been busted for drugs and word was they couldn't get visas. Brian Jones, the actual founder of the Stones, showed up in Monterey anyway and was all over the place, looking very way out.

The headliners for the first night were Simon and Garfunkel, and I always liked listening to them. To me they were kind of like the Odd Couple. Short, serious, clever Paul Simon, who usually looked worried about something, with straight brown hair cut schoolboy short, and Art Garfunkel, who towered over little Paul and had a mop of blonde curly hair, probably not as smart as Paul, but a better singer with a beautiful voice, and who just about always looked annoyed with

Paul for something or other. They'd actually met when they were boys back at Public School 164 in Flushing, Queens, and I later found out Paul saw Art singing in a fourth-grade talent show, liked his voice, and figured if he teamed up it might help him meet girls. That was why I wanted to sing in that garage band, too! One thing about moving from a mixed neighborhood in Riverside up to an all white area near Sacramento was it exposed me to music I might not have heard. It kind of forced you to open up to new styles, and at Del Campo High I kept hearing about "The Sound of Silence," released in 1964, and was curious about these two guys. Art Garfunkel reminded me of a Jewish kid I knew at Del Campo named Andy Samuels, who we called Brillo. They had the same look. I found Simon and Garfunkel's music intriguing. They had real good voices and understood harmony, and if you paid attention to the words, you knew those dudes were deep. That was why I tuned in at that time. You didn't just rock out. You knew every word to almost every song.

At Monterey John Phillips came out to introduce them, wearing some kind of Russian fur hat or something, and referred to Simon and Garfunkel as "two people who, in the music business, are respected by everyone," and that was true. They walked out on stage looking kind of like Beatniks, you know, both of them in turtleneck sweaters, Paul Simon holding a guitar that would be all the accompaniment they needed. They opened with "Homeward Bound," which I knew, and a new song I'd never heard before, then did that whole "Feelin' Groovy" thing that, even then, seemed almost a little silly or something, but at the same time, it was cool. They really got going with "The Sound of Silence." Man, that was intense. Garfunkel was singing his ass off and those are some deep lyrics, even if to this day I don't know what they're talking about exactly. "People writing songs that voices never share"? "And the people bowed and prayed to the neon god they made"? Say what? It didn't matter. The crowd was into it, Gary and I were into it, and by the time they played their encore and wrapped up, we were fired up for the next two days of the concert.

We slept in the car that night and went down to the beach in the morning. We kind of strolled over toward the ocean, though there was no way we were going in there. It was too cold! The fog had settled in overnight and wasn't going anywhere that morning, so it was just over 50 degrees. Gary and I kind of pretended like we'd come out of the water and went over to the showers and lathered up. It was fun. Part of that feeling of pure freedom that kept us feeling great all weekend.

I later became such a fan of the Canned Heat, an L.A. blues band that liked to get down and boogie, John Lee Hooker style, that I went down to Mexico for winter ball one year with only two re-cords, and one was Creedence Clearwater Revival and the other was the Canned Heat. I wore that vinyl out! But if Gary and I made it to the Monterey fairgrounds on Saturday in time to see the Heat, it didn't make much of an impression on either of us. But we were there for Big Brother and the Holding Company. I loved Big Brother and the Holding Company. And any time you saw Janis Joplin perform live, that made an impression. Chet Helms, who introduced them, was big in the whole San Francisco music scene, in fact he was the "Big Brother" of the name and the guy who had encour-aged Janis to join the group.

"Three or four years ago, on one of my peren-nial hitchhikes across the country," he told the crowd in Monterey, for his introduction, "I ran into a chick from Texas by the name of Janis Joplin. I heard her sing, and Janis and I hitchhiked to the West Coast in fifty hours, probably the fastest trip across the country we ever made. A lot of things have gone down since, but it gives me a lot of pride today to present the finished product, Big Brother and the Holding Company."

They opened with "Down on Me," a traditional song they'd written new words to that year, and played a very out there, psychedelic set, finishing with a version of the Big Mama Thornton tune "Ball and Chain" that was as trippy as it was bluesy. When Janis sang words like "sitting down by my window/ jus' lookin' out at the rain," she sang like someone who had grown up on the blues the way that I had. She didn't sing like a white girl. When she sang "Why does everything go wrong?" you had no doubt she was singing about her own experiences. She didn't hold anything back, not a damn thing. Any time I saw Janis sing, and that was not the only time I caught her, it left me feeling both jacked up and kind of exhausted. That was how intense it was listening to her. At Monterey when she finished "Ball and Chain," Big Mama

Cass was sitting up near the front, shaking her head and just mouthing "Wow."

"It was as if the earth had opened up," Joel Selvin wrote in his excellent book, called *Monterey Pop*, which I highly recommend if you can track down a copy. It's a collector's item! "Her voice commanded the ear. She vibrated from deep within. Once she opened her mouth and sang, this otherwise unprepossessing person seemed to grow taller before the audience's eyes. ... The audience was spellbound, startled at the crude power unleashed, and they rocked the arena with cheers and applause. She was the first real hit of the festival, a taste of what everybody had come to see. Janis Joplin had raised the stakes of the game."

The day was such a kaleidoscope of impressions, even that day or that week it was all jumbled together with no way to sort it all out. Gary and I would walk around, letting our eyes wander. It wasn't the kind of scene Woodstock would be later, where most everyone there was a hippie dressed as hippie as they could get. You had all kinds of young people at Monterey, some of them looking straight as could be, in little button-down shirts and nice pants, but you also had people who were deep into what was happening in San Francisco and L.A., with their love beads and their wild hairdos, their big, funky hats and their red-white-and-blue, mock-the-flag outfits, their jerky, drugged-out way of dancing, like chickens being electrocuted. The smell of grass was everywhere and people would kind of lounge around on the big lawns, smoking a joint, taking it easy. Gary and I were athletes and at that time I was not about to mess around with no marijuana. I had a pact with Dennis that we took very seriously: Absolutely no grass! I was on a mission to make something of my future and that was going to take dedication to training my body, I knew. But the truth was, even if you weren't inhaling, there was so much of the stuff in the air you almost had to get some kind of contact high going. The beautiful part was, it was see and be seen, but all in such a low-key way, like it didn't matter who you were, it didn't matter how you looked, it just mattered that you were there and taking in what was going down, which we all knew even that weekend was something people would be talking about for a lot of years to come.

We were giddy hearing that much good music, such a variety of styles, so much of it cutting edge.

This was wild stuff that made you thrill at what music could be. It felt so good to be young, soaking everything up like a sponge, at a time when there was so much to soak up. Janis pretty much walked away with Saturday, but you also had Country Joe McDonald, his face done up in war paint, and the Fish. That was a band I knew from my drives into Berkeley, and they came through with their famous anti-war song.

And it's one, two, three, what are we
fighting for?
Don't ask me I don't give a damn
Next stop is Vietnam.
And it's five, six, seven, open up the
pearly gates,
Well there ain't no time to wonder why,
Whoopie! We're all gonna die!

Later came the Butterfield Blues Band, and I was a fan of Paul Butterfield. This was foot-stompin' old-time blues like my daddy would listen to, tunes like their own "Born in Chicago" and Johnny Moore's "Driftin' Blues." The funny thing about that day is Elvin Bishop was putting on a show with his guitar work — there are pictures of him up on stage — and I didn't have the first idea of Elvin at the time. I had not heard of him. I knew the guitarist with the mop of curly hair sure could play, but I didn't know his name then. Later, we became good friends, which we are to this day.

Elvin told me all about what it was like to be a musician at Monterey. Just getting there was pretty crazy, he told me. He was on the same small plane as Steve Cropper and Otis Redding's band. The small airport was socked in with fog, so they circled and circled, waiting for it to clear, and finally the pilot announced: "The fog is not clearing, so we're just going to have to take a chance." They went in for a landing and, Elvin remembers, "We fell like two hundred feet in a second. I looked over at the guy next to me and his cup of coffee was about five feet long." They were all happy to get out of the plane and join in the fun backstage at Monterey.

"It was great, man. I got to see all these people I'd been wanting to see for a long time. There were a lot of firsts at that concert. A lot of people that became icons nationally burst into the consciousness there, like Janis Joplin and Otis Redding and Hendrix. I used to jam with Hendrix in New York quite a bit. He was a real nice guy, very soft spoken, a considerate guy, not personally flamboyant at all the way he was on stage."

I felt like my musical education, listening to my father's music all those years, was really paying off. Quicksilver Messenger Service, one of the top San Francisco bands of the era, came out for a set and closed with Bo Diddley's "Who Do You Love?" Steve Miller Band, another one I'd catch many times, did a fun little number called "Mercury Blues," all about buying a Mercury and cruising up and down the road. How about a Rambler?

There were more than 30,000 people gathered in the fairgrounds area by the time that evening's concert opened with Tom Smothers of *The Smothers Brothers* TV program introducing Moby Grape, another psychedelic band out of San Francisco, followed by Hugh Masekela, from South Africa, who played jazz trumpet — and happened to be a favorite of my mother's. She loved him, but the kids in Monterey were unimpressed. I guess they just weren't ready to dig Hugh Masekela. The Byrds played a set, including a cover of Dylan's

"Chimes of Freedom" and then their song "So You Wanna Be A Rock 'n' Roll Star," basically making fun of the made-for-TV Monkees, but they didn't really strike a chord either.

That was all cool, but the electricity kicked in when Jerry Garcia of the Grateful Dead introduced the Jefferson Airplane as his idea of "a perfect example of what the world is coming to." The Airplane were the ultimate San Francisco psychedelic band as far as I was concerned, after seeing them the month before in Santa Clara, and their second album, *Surrealistic Pillow*, had just made it to the Top Ten. At Monterey they jumped right into one of their hits from that album, "Somebody to Love," and just tore it up. Grace Slick was a former model and she had stage presence, but above all she could flat-out sing. She belted it out. Their third song that night was "White Rabbit," and it would go Top Ten and be a famous song and all, but as much as people might understand that it's about psychedelic drugs, inspired by Lewis Carroll's nineteenth-century *Alice's Adventures in Wonderland* and *Through the Looking-Glass*, it was also inspired by Miles Davis and musically it's a song that has a sustained intensity that carries you right through. That song was some wild ride! I was digging them. I was all ears, if you know what I mean.

Closing out the night was the great Otis Redding. As the guy says in *Animal House*, "Otis, my man!" Otis *was* the man. He was one of my dad's favorites and *of course* he was! It wasn't just his voice, which had to have been one of the smoothest ever, he was a musician's musician, brilliant and driven, and he was just on another plane from most everyone else. At Monterey he came out in a bright outfit (Was that green? Teal? Who knew?) and got the place rocking with Sam Cooke's "Shake." For me it was all just what I'd expect, because Otis knew how to put on a show, but some of the people in the crowd had never heard of Otis and they didn't know what hit them! "Shake! Everybody say it! Shake! Let me hear the whole crowd!" It was electric.

One of the most popular songs in the country that week was "Respect" as sung by Aretha Franklin, which would hit No. 1 the following week. Otis wrote the song, as I well knew, but it was a revelation for most of the people in Monterey to hear the Otis version. After that he looked out at the thousands of people jammed in to the arena and said, "This is the love crowd, right? We all love each other, don't we? Am I right? Let me hear you say 'Yeah!'" Then he sang "I've Been Loving You Too Long," a slower number he seemed to slow down even more, and bounced around on stage to his own version of "Satisfaction" by the Rolling Stones, and closed his twenty-minute set with "Try a Little Tenderness," a song that had already been covered by both Bing Crosby and Frank Sinatra, introducing it, "This is a song I want to dedicate to all the miniskirts." This was soul music, at its best, backed up by Booker T. and the M.G.'s with Steve Cropper's guitar and the show-stopping drumming of Al Jackson Jr., as well as the Mar-Keys horn section. The crowd was mesmerized. They didn't want him to leave. "I got to go, y'all," he told them, making his way off stage. "I don't wanna go." That trippy, playful psychedelic stuff was great fun, but this was music that stuck to your ribs, music that made you *feel* and keep feelin'. After that they all knew who Otis was.

That was the first time I saw Otis perform and I was hooked. I couldn't wait to see him again. That December he recorded a cut called "(Sittin'

On) The Dock of the Bay," which he'd started
writing that year during a stay in Sausalito, just
across from San Francisco. Otis was due to come
back to California for some concerts and I had
tickets to see him at a gig in San Francisco. But
on December 9, 1967, the twin engine Beechcraft
H18 carrying him to a gig in Madison, Wisconsin,
crashed into Lake Monona, killing Redding and
most of the band. Otis Redding, one of the greatest
singers this country has ever produced, was dead
at age twenty-six. "(Sittin' On) The Dock of the Bay"
was released a month later and went straight to
No. 1, selling more than four million copies. There
were a lot of deaths in those years, buddies I went
to school with who died in Vietnam, the assassina-
tions of Malcolm in 1965 and Martin Luther King
Jr. and Bobby Kennedy in 1968, but the death of
Otis so young, so full of promise, so ready to make
more beautiful music to make our lives better and
sweeter, that haunts me to this day. A year or so
ago, I went down to Lompoc to see a friend and
went over to Morro Bay, walked out on a dock
and just sat there staring out at the water, thinking about Otis. I sat there for two hours. In a way
I feel like I'm still sitting there, I'll always be sitting

there, staring out at the water with the sound of
Otis Redding singing about the dock of the bay
ringing in my ears and tugging at my heart.

Chapter 4
Wild Thing

The third day of the Monterey Pop Festival started with Ravi Shankar playing the sitar, and I'm sure it was cool and all, but Gary and I didn't catch Ravi. I mean no disrespect. It was a big deal when George Harrison of the Beatles flew all the way to Bombay, India, one year earlier to study with Shankar, who was one of the top musicians in India and internationally famous. I'm open to all kinds of music and the complexity and artistry of sitar music might be just the thing in another mood. I'm not sure what mood that would be. Some mood. But that weekend was all about groovin' and rockin' out.

The evening concert opened with the Blues Project, white guys from Greenwich Village playing the blues, and then it was Big Brother and the Holding Company back out on stage. Gary and

I were like: Didn't we see them yesterday? Didn't Janis Joplin *nail* it? They were back, I found out later, for D.A. Pennebaker. He was the dude who had already done a Bob Dylan documentary called *Don't Look Back* and he had cameras rolling in Monterey. For some reason he hadn't filmed Janis the day before, so they were going to do it all again, and we got to hear her sing her guts out on "Ball and Chain" one more time. Pennebaker produced a great documentary on Monterey, by the way. I watch it now and I feel like I'm back there in the moment, seeing it all for the first time, so the film was a huge help in pulling together my memories for this book.

I was looking forward to seeing the Buffalo Springfield, who had got together in L.A. the year before. Stephen Stills and some other musicians looking to form a band were on Sunset Boulevard when they happened to spot Neil Young driving the other way in his black hearse and turned around to follow him. Neil Young didn't make it to Monterey, since he'd quit the band shortly before, but David Crosby played with them instead, and they jumped right into "For What It's Worth," written and sung by Stills, which had been a hit for them earlier that year. It was another of those anthem-of-the-'60s type songs and I'm glad I got to see Stills sing it, standing toward the front of the stage with big, bushy, reddish-blonde sideburns. It's the one that keeps repeating "It's time we stop, hey, what's that sound/ Everybody look what's going down" and talks about:

What a field-day for the heat
A thousand people in the street
Singing songs and carrying signs
Mostly say, hooray for our side

What none of us knew there in the crowd was that as Buffalo Springfield was performing, there was some tension backstage. Neither Jimi Hendrix nor the Who wanted to follow the other. It's hard to say just what went down, but here's how Joel Selvin summed it up in his book: "Backstage, Pete Townshend of the Who angrily confronted Jimi Hendrix. He accused Hendrix of stealing his act, and the two argued about who would follow who. Townshend was still smarting from the experience of having followed Hendrix earlier in the year at London's Saville Theatre. Phillips resolved the matter with a flip of the coin, and the Who went on first." Phillips later insisted that Townshend and Hendrix had almost come to blows, and I tell you what, I'd take Jimi in any scuffle between those two. Phillips also said that once the flip went against him, "Jimi jumped up on a chair and yelled that if he was going to follow the Who, he was going to pull out all the stops and blow everybody away."

I didn't know much about the Who then, but then at that point I wasn't really aware of Hendrix either. The Who came out of London, and they had an edgy emotional intensity that was light years away from the whole trippy jam-band style of a lot of the new music in San Francisco. Roger Daltrey was the lead singer and front man, a good-looking guy with the kind of face sure to appeal to teenage girls, and hard-pounding drummer Keith Moon and phenomenally fast bassist John Entwistle were key to the sound, but the personality of the Who had everything to do with guitarist Pete Townshend, the guy with the hang-dog look and long nose, kind of like Snoop Dogg before Snoop Dogg. Townshend wrote the songs and it was his edgy presence and fierce intelligence that made the Who so different.

At Monterey the Who opened with "Substitute," a whole song riffing on one word from the line "Although she may be cute she's just a substitute" from the great Smokey Robinson's "The Tracks of My Tears." Gary and I were like: *What is this?* They were singing in harmony, so in some ways it wasn't so different from some of the San Francisco rock we'd been hearing all weekend, but Moon's drumming was as subtle as the sound of a bowling ball bouncing down a wood stairwell. I mean that as a compliment. Wham! Wham! Wham! He was just wailing away, but underneath that beat was the spidery quick bass work of Entwistle, which leaped around like mad but stayed right in the groove. They followed "Substitute" up with a little Eddie Cochran rockabilly number, "Summertime Blues," which everyone enjoyed ("Ain't no cure for the Summertime Blues!") and a Townshend song "Pictures of Lilly," all about discovering as a boy the pleasures of looking at pinup girls.

The only Who song I'd heard before was "My Generation," but catching it on the radio was nothing like hearing them close their set in Monterey with it. It had been a Top Ten hit all over Europe, though it only rose to No. 74 on the U.S. charts. At Monterey it had a pogo-stick, bouncing energy that lifted everyone up, especially when Daltrey sang "I hope I die before I get old!" That line went over real well with the kids in Monterey. From there everyone was paying more attention as the band pounded away and Daltrey stuttered for effect.

"Why don't you all fade away?" he sang, and then the band behind sang "Talkin' 'bout my generation."

"And don't try to dig what we all say," and again, "Talkin' 'bout my generation."

"I'm not trying to cause a big ssss-sensation," and "Talkin' 'bout my generation."

"I'm just talkin' bout my g-g-generation," and "Talkin' 'bout my generation."

I know that nowadays it's gotten to be kind of a cliché, playing up the unprecedented uniqueness of every single generation that comes along. Generation X and Generation Y. I don't know what any of that is supposed to mean. But we were the Baby Boom, born after World War II, there were a lot of us and the technology of communication was shifting quickly as we moved into the television age. At the time the idea of youth culture upending everything felt new and fresh. It sounded deep to talk about "my generation," which was why everyone was talking about it all the time. Only Townshend and the Who turned the idea into music like that.

But it wasn't just the words or the sound: Townshend was putting on a show. I'll let Joel Selvin describe it to you. "Townshend underlined the song's lyrical message with guitar playing that sounded like a street fight, punctuated by haymaker drumming from Keith Moon," he wrote in *Monterey Pop*. "With the guitar roaring of its own accord, smoke bombs went off at the rear of the stage, the clouds obscuring the psychedelic light show. Townshend stood like a crane, his arms outstretched, guitar swinging in front of him. He sawed the strings against the mike stand, took off the strap and flipped the guitar around over his head. Then, suddenly, violently, he began to smash the instrument against the stage like a sledgehammer. He knocked over a mike stand, and a stagehand racing to preserve the equipment nearly lost his head to Townshend's guitar."

It's strange to think of Jerry Garcia, probably one of the greatest guitarists ever, as almost an afterthought, but in a way that was how it was at Monterey. The Grateful Dead came out for a set, almost an intermission between the Who and what was next — the Jimi Hendrix Experience — and this was back in the days when the Dead were something new. They'd formed in Palo Alto just two years earlier, and this was the early lineup with Ron "Pigpen" McKernan as the first front man. Pigpen's whole thing was the blues. His father was one of the few white DJs to work at KDIA, a top soul and funk station in the Bay Area through the 1960s and '70s, and he sang songs for the Dead like Bobby Bland's "Turn On Your Love Light." Monterey was my first time hearing the Dead and at first I didn't know what to make of them. They played a song called "Cold Rain and Snow" in a place where it never snowed, let alone in June, but I do remember Garcia getting my attention with some very energetic guitar work. It was like you had to pay constant attention to what he was doing because he could veer in one of several different directions. And their songs went on and on and on, and if you were digging them, and by then I was, that was very cool.

I almost had to laugh when I saw Jimi come out for his set. He was wearing a headband, and had a feather boa draped around his neck and shoulders, glowing red or pink in the stage lights. His costume included a black vest, orange ruffled shirt, bright pants and some kind of exotic jacket over all of that with heavy chains and metal pendant hanging on his chest, making Jimi look part gypsy, part pirate captain, part maharaja. Then he started playing and literally from the first seconds it just seized you right away that history was being made. I've been around for a lot of heavy stuff. I know that a lot of times when something major is going down, you're not even aware of that at the time. But some stuff you just know. Like seven years later in Atlanta, on April 8, 1974, I was kneeling in the on-deck circle when Hank Aaron hit his record-setting 715th home run: You knew that was a moment you'd remember your whole life. It was like that with Hendrix in Monterey as well.

There was something both demonic and angelic in his intensity in going to work on his Fender Stratocaster, which he played upside down and backwards, being left-handed. This was live music, no overdubbing, but it sounded like about four different dudes had to be all playing at once to explain all the sound coming from Jimi's guitar. How did he *do* that? Sometimes watching him you had the feeling that the guitar was playing him rather than the other way around, because no mortal could do so many different things. Like, even before he started singing any of the words to the first song they played at Monterey, a speeded-up version of "Killing Floor" by Howlin' Wolf, already he lifted his strumming hand up into the air and let his left hand on the bridge of the guitar noodle around with a brief burst of howling, careening, freeform guitar-solo pyrotechnics.

Hendrix was born in Seattle in 1942, so he was just seven years older than me, and we were both given the same name at birth, but he spelled it wrong (Johnny). He'd kicked around in his teens, playing backup for Little Richard and who knew who else, but the two things to know about him were that he'd spent some time in Greenwich Village, soaking up the influence of some heavy songwriters like the young Bob Dylan, and then went over to England and joined up with two English guys, drummer Mitch Mitchell and bassist Noel Redding, to form the Jimi Hendrix Experience. Mitchell and Redding both had mops of curly hair and Jimi liked to kid that Redding looked like Bob Dylan's grandmother.

Mitchell at Monterey was on fire, giving what had to be one of the great performances of his life. He was pounding almost as hard as Keith Moon, but mixing in all kinds of cascading sound, working so hard to keep up with Jimi he reminded me of a guy moving his feet all over the floor to try to play shut-down defense on a stud like Elgin Baylor. The three played in sync and Redding and Mitchell brought out the best in Jimi; he loved playing his colorful personality against their straighter looks, though they were doing their best with the costuming, too. They'd had some hits in England, but this was the first time I tuned into them and all I could do was grin and shake my head.

Introducing the second song, "Foxy Lady," Jimi called out "What's happening?" and then talked directly to the crowd in a low-key, conversational way, almost like he was both up on stage and hanging with us, too. "My fingers won't move, as you see, you won't hear no sounds, but dig this," he said, and then the speakers exploded with the pulsating power of Jimi's Stratocaster. Now remember, my dad raised me on the blues. I knew my blues. I'd listened to all the same music that had inspired Jimi, Howlin' Wolf and B.B. King and on and on. I was also a young guy in Northern California, so I'd heard some of the music experiments, the fooling around with technology to create way-out sound. I knew what I was hearing and that was a guy who could give his music a crackle and growl and scream, could detonate it like a stack of dynamite, but do it all *in* the music, *in* the groove, true to the integrity of his musical sources.

And best of all, he was having himself one heck of a great time, grinning at the pure joy of playing, chomping away on some gum, sticking his tongue out again and again, and talking to us in the crowd like we were his best friends.

"Hey baby, what's happening?" he said after "Foxy Lady," pointing down at someone in the front of the crowd, laughing, and soon everyone was laughing along with him. The place was buzzing like the crowd gathered in Florida for the launch of one of those giant Apollo Saturn V rockets that would take us to the moon. "Dig, I tell you what, let's get down to business. Just give me one second to get down to business. I've got to keep people honest, dig this. Yeah dig brother, it's really out of sight here. It didn't even rain. No buttons to push. And right now I'd like to dedicate this song to everybody here with hearts, any kind of hearts and ears."

"Ex-cuse me," he continued after more crazy-ass cool guitar work, his voice tripping on the "'cuse" like a kid going through puberty and hitting a sudden high note, but it was just because he was excited and having so much fun. "Excuse me for a minute and just let me play my guitar, all right?" he said. "Right now I'd like to do a thing by Bob Dylan. That's his grandma over there. It's a little thing called 'Like a Rolling Stone.'"

And play he did. Man! I'm *still* trippin' on it all these years later. Now as far as the actual singing, I loved it but it was nothing my mother would have liked, since half the time Jimi was talking as much as he was singing, but the energy and the raw sonic force of the music were just off the charts. The song ended and all around were kids who loved Dylan, a lot of them looking pretty straight, at least compared to the scene at Woodstock two years later, and they were holding up their hands to clap wildly, needing to show they knew they were part of something amazing and timeless.

Playing "Rock Me Baby," a blues tune performed by B.B. King and others, Hendrix let his own lead vocals compete with the wailing of his lead guitar. Jimi's guitar could talk and sing. It could do most anything. Midway through the song he let fly with a solo where his guitar was wailing, and each time he'd throw his picking hand up in the air, and finally he held the strings up to his mouth and started playing with his teeth. In "Hey Joe," up next, he took off on a solo that a lot of us will always know by heart. How do you try to describe something like that with words? Making the Strat purr and screech and then climbing the stairs with a series of raw power chords to pull it to a close. He brought a tenderness to singing "The Wind Cries Mary," which he wrote, and even his guitar playing was low key through much of the tune, showing the crowd he could take it down a notch.

When I think back on it now, the look on Jimi's face between songs that day was a look I know all too well: It was the look of someone who has just hit a home run. To fans the feeling you have when you hit a home run must seem like the ultimate in self-congratulation or exultation, and there is some of that in there, especially with certain homers, but most of all the feeling you have is a kind of calm exhilaration and wonder, a sense not that you had *done* something in launching that ball over the fence but that you were *part* of something, the swing of your bat striking a ball rushing your way and connecting to make something special happen. You almost feel that the bat did the work, it feels so light in your hands, the swing feels so easy. Hendrix had that exhilarated look of being as amazed as all of us at what was happening with his guitar. And I know he had some chemical help with that exhilaration, but what you saw was a childlike joyousness and ease, a sense of complete comfort, since he knew he was tapping into major talent and everyone else there knew it, too, including Michelle Phillips and Mama Cass and the other fellow musicians all watching from the front row, as blown away as the rest of us. That was even more so when Jimi kicked into another of his own songs, "Purple Haze," which he always insisted was a love song, though everyone else thought it was about getting high.

Purple Haze all in my brain,
lately things don't seem the same,
actin' funny but I don't know why
'scuse me while I kiss the sky.

Yes, we were all kissing the sky, all of us gathered there for Jimi that night — and it felt great. Last up was a song called "Wild Thing," which an English band called the Troggs had turned into a No. 1 hit the year before, but Jimi was in no hurry to get started. He was a showman and he was having himself a great time, so why not drag it out a little? He looked out at the crowd, grinning.

"This is something else, man," he said. "It isn't no

big story about how you know we couldn't make it here, so we go over to England and America doesn't like us 'cause our feet's too big, or we got fat mattresses and we wear golden underwear," he said in that same playful, low-key style. "It ain't no scene like that, brother. Dig, man, I was laying around and I went to England and picked up these two cats and now here we are, man. It was so groovy to come back this way and really get a chance to really play."

He sounded like a kid opening up presents on Christmas morning, so much joy was coming through.

"I could sit up here all night and say thank you, thank you, thank you," he continued. "I wish I could just grab you, man, and just oooh" — and here he reached his arms out, as if to grab, and his tongue darted out — "one of them things, one of those scenes. But dig, I just can't do that. So what I'm gonna do, I'm gonna sacrifice something right here that I really love — thank you very much, Bob Dylan's grandmother. Anyway, I'm going to sacrifice something I really love, man. Don't think I'm silly doing this, you know, 'cause I don't think I'm losing my mind. Last night, man, ooh God. ... Wait — wait a minute. But today I think it's the right thing, all

right. So I'm not losing my mind. This is for everybody here. This is the only way I can do it. So we're
gonna do the English and American combined anthem together. Don't get mad. Noooo. Don't get mad.
I want everybody to join in, too, all right? Don't get
mad. This is it, man. There's nothing I can do more
than this. Oooh, look at those beautiful people
out there."

If some of the others in the crowd knew what
Jimi was talking about, Gary and I sure had no idea.
But it was all pretty wild, man. Jimi ripped that
song up and then played a long, crazy solo, picking
hand held high up in the air, and kept bending notes
all over the place, then actually went down on his
knees, played some more, and rolled into a back-
ward somersault right there on the stage, playing
his guitar the whole time without interruption or in-
cident. Later he had the guitar behind his back and
kept playing it there, grinning and winking into the
crowd as if that were the easiest, most natural thing
in the world to do. Then he started running toward
the back of the stage, pumping his hips against the
guitar and holding it toward the big speakers to get
more feedback. The man was humping his guitar!
Then he hopped out toward the front of the stage,

down on his knees with the guitar between his legs, pointed toward the crowd, and played and pumped some more.

It was like some kind of ceremony. He was holding one hand up in the air, like a bull rider, and plucking away with the other, pulling raw sound out of the guitar, and then he finally just let go and let the sound growl on its own for a moment and held his hands in front and moved his fingers like he was running them through sand. Then it was like: What is he doing? He had a little bottle in his hand and squirted something onto the guitar, then leaned over and kissed it. What? Huh? Then he lit a match and tossed it down and his guitar was on fire! Right there on stage. He squirted more of what must have been lighter fluid on it and urged the flames upward with his outstretched fingertips, then squirted some more and waved his hands up some more. Through all this the speakers were blaring with the sound of the thrumming guitar burning. Finally he jumped up and swung the guitar all over the place, missing the mark a couple of times it looked to me, and slamming it down squarely against the stage, snapping it. And through it all Mitch Mitchell was pounding away on the drums, Jimi was tossing fragments of the busted guitar into the crowd and then suddenly they were gone. The look in the crowd was more shock than appreciation. They didn't know what had hit them. I didn't either.

Chapter 5
Decision Time

'd been into music my whole life, but I'd never seen anything like Jimi Hendrix in that outfit of his up on stage in Monterey putting on a show like that, doing more with a guitar than anyone would have believed if they didn't see it with their own eyes. I'll never forget watching him set fire to the thing in some crazy ceremony of joy and intense commitment. As I said earlier, I went down to Monterey with really no idea about Jimi Hendrix. He just wasn't on my radar. But after Monterey, he became my new fascination. I couldn't stop talkin' about Jimi. He stole the show, to me.

Back home near Sacramento just after Monterey, there was a lot of talk about what had gone down over the weekend, and once again I had to thank my mother for giving me those tickets and putting me at the center of the action. The Jimi Hendrix Experience followed up after Monterey with five straight concerts at the Fillmore the following week and then gave a free outdoor concert that Sunday afternoon in the Panhandle of Golden Gate Park, right in the heart of San Francisco's Haight-Ashbury district, where the whole Summer of Love thing was going down. I'd have loved to be there, but Mama did not offer me the Rambler. Jimi went down to L.A. after that, playing a gig at the Whiskey a Go-Go, where Jim Morrison and the Doors were still regulars at that point, and then spent July and August doing a lot of gigs back East, especially in New York, and then that was it, no more Jimi in the U.S. until early the following year.

After Monterey I kept playing Jimi for friends, sometimes almost forcing them to listen, and some of them would dig it and some others would stare at me and give me a funny look. "Man," one friend would ask me, "Why do you like that?" Why *did* I like that so much? I don't know exactly. I can just say it mesmerized me and put me in a kind of trance, it was so different from anything I'd ever heard. It was frightening, in its way, and I didn't understand it, but I was attracted to it and I always wanted to hear more of it.

This cat was so out there, the straight world had no idea what to make of him, and that was part of the fun. Jimi's name showed up in the pages of the *New York Times*, which was as establishment as it got, just a few months after I saw him in Monterey, and it's funny to look back now at that article, which was published under the heading "A Genuine Nightmare." "The Jimi Hendrix Experience is neither a pill nor a weed, but three young musicians who came over from England recently and gained notoriety with a stage act that's reputedly enough to make a sailor blush," Tom Phillips wrote on November 12, 1967. Do sailors blush? I know the Marines I served with sure didn't.

Phillips goes on to tell readers that the album cover of *Are You Experienced* "reinforces the degeneracy theme," with Jimi and his two bandmates looking like "surrealistic hermaphrodites." Surrealistic, sure, all the way. But Jimi a hermaphrodite? You gotta be kiddin' me. Ain't no dude ever enjoyed being with women — one, several — more than Jimi Hendrix. "It comes as a real surprise to find that the disk itself is a serious nightmare show," Tom Phillips continues, "with genuine lust and misery; and also a highly successful blending of simple folk-blues and forms with advanced electronic sound effects."

So the dude *liked* what he was hearing? He just didn't want to come out and say that up front in the *New York Times* so he had to throw all that other stuff out there first. But once he got going, he was an entertaining writer.

"Noel Redding plays a bass guitar with the amplification tuned up so far that it's a bit haywire most of the time — it sounds like a cello, bowed with a hacksaw and fed through a bullhorn," he tells us, then concludes with this thumbs up: "The sound is robust and hellish and tightly controlled; and Hendrix, who writes the lyrics, knows what he's writing about."

*   *   *

The summer of '67 was a strange and thrilling and challenging time for me. I liked the freedom that came with no longer having my dad around, at least not at the house, but at the same time I missed having him around. I wanted to think that at age eighteen I had all the answers, but I knew I needed some help in trying to get my head straight. The Braves had drafted me so low, I didn't think I wanted to sign a contract with them, which in those years meant I'd be considered a professional in all sports, so could never play college basketball or football, not even run track. I was more focused on going to Santa Clara to play basketball and baseball, or maybe somewhere else, like San Jose State or Arizona State University. I loved the idea of being a star athlete at a big university, being the big man on campus with everything that came with that.

I was playing American Legion baseball that summer, but figured I'd have time once the season ran its course to go play football and basketball before I had to make a decision on college or professional baseball. I was lucky that summer to have a great coach. His name was Spider Jorgensen and he knew just how to get the most out of me. He was easy-going. He was always soft-spoken and never yelled. He didn't *tell* you what to do, he kind of suggested that you do this or you do that. That's what the good coaches do, I've learned, they suggest, rather than tell you, because if you *tell* someone everything they're supposed to do, it's just human nature to want to reject that.

When I took over as manager of the San Francisco Giants in 1993, my first time as a manager, my bench coach, Bob Lillis, taught me that lesson all over again — and it was the best thing that ever happened to me. Every young manager should have a veteran bench coach. He's not a threat to you. He's there as a resource and he's going to help you so much you're going to have probably more respect for him than anybody else. Bob had a great way of giving me a gentle nudge without pointing out how far off I was. He wouldn't shoot my idea down. He'd just make some other suggestion, starting it out with "Did you ever consider …?" That was how I knew if I was borderline wrong or just plain wrong. That was when I knew I was about to do something messed up.

"Do you think I should hit and run right now, Bob?" I'd ask him.

He'd pause, look at me for a minute, then answer: "Did you ever consider a straight steal?" Or: "Did you ever consider a sacrifice bunt?"

Bob would never tell me what to do, and that was Spider Jorgensen's style, too. Above all he was a good listener. He paid attention. He understood that I'd had a rough senior year at Del Campo in baseball. A lot of big-league ball clubs were scouting me and I let it throw me off. I was trying to impress the scouts. Coach Jorgensen never said anything to me, he never gave me any sense that he was aware of my situation and looking for a way forward for me, he just focused on taking every day as it came, every game as it came, and putting me in a position to be my best. He helped straighten me out that summer playing American Legion ball for him in Fair Oaks.

A funny thing about Coach Jorgensen: I knew he was a good coach. I knew he knew the game. He had all kinds of drills he would do with us that were better than anything I'd seen before. Like his favorite was to give you a broom and have you swing full out like you were swinging at a ball. The first time I saw soft toss was with Spider and that's something I used all through my time in pro ball and I'm still using it today with my son. Coach Jorgensen cared about you and he cared about the game, but he didn't care about trying to impress anyone. He never once mentioned to me or any of us that he'd played in the big leagues.

Years later, after eight seasons with the Braves, they traded me to the Dodgers before the 1976 season. I remember my first spring training with the Dodgers, I was there at Dodgertown in Vero Beach, Florida, checking out a big mural. It was very cool. So much Dodgers history. There was Roy

Campanella and Gil Hodges and of course Jackie Robinson. I read underneath and saw a caption at the far end of the mural talking about "Spider Jorgensen" tagging someone out at third base. Say what? I didn't know what to think, so I called my dad.

"Did Spider ever play for the Dodgers?" I asked him.

"Oh yeah," he said.

"He never told me that," I said.

"You never asked," my dad said.

It was true. I never did. Not only had Spider played for the Dodgers, he'd been teammates with Jackie Robinson. They made their major-league debuts on the same day, April 15, 1947, a great day for this country. In fact, if you go see that movie *42*, all about Jackie, there's a Spider Jorgensen character, since he was one of the players who reached out to Jackie and tried to support him. In the movie they showed Jackie going over to third to talk to Spider. I was like: Damn, Spider played with Jackie? If I'd have known that, I'd have asked him a thousand questions.

Through most of the summer of '67, I had no idea what I was going to do with my future. Things were in turmoil with our family. That extra three hundred dollars a month that my dad had to pay for his place had to be made up somehow. I prayed on it, like, "What am I supposed to do?"

A part of me thought there was no way I was going to sign with the Braves. I didn't want to go to the South. We'd watch TV together and see the Freedom Marches. We'd see dogs and fire hoses being used on anyone who was sympathetic to the cause. I heard that some people in the Braves organization were worried that I wasn't serious about playing baseball, since I was a four-sport athlete and clearly loved those other sports as well. Did I really love baseball? I didn't like hearing that much at all. What did love have to do with it? They either thought I had potential as a player or they did not. If they paid me to come play for them, I was going to give my all and nobody would be talking about whether I loved the game or not. That was if they paid me, not if they *insulted* me.

I was leaning toward college, but no option I tried to imagine ever felt totally right. If I tried to go with my gut, and let it point me toward the truth of what I needed to do, all I ended up with was a stomachache. I was just going to have to wait and see how things played out. I had American Legion baseball and then once that was over, I'd go play some football or basketball or both. In football I'd made an all-star team for Northern California sponsored by the Optimist Club and was looking forward to playing on that team against Southern California. I'd also been chosen for a basketball all-star team that was going to play some games in Mexico. And I had already gone to the state finals in track and field to do the long jump.

Coach Jorgensen did a great job getting us ready and the team kept winning. I thought about leaving my team to go play in Mexico with that all-star basketball team, which would have been some kind of adventure, or to play in that all-star football game, but leaving my teammates in the lurch just wasn't something I was capable of doing. We won the North Division championship and advanced to the state American Legion playoffs in mid-August, which were held at the Veterans Home of California in Yountville in Napa Valley, about an hour and a half from home. That was close enough that all our homeboys came out, a lot of parents, girls cheering us on. It was a wild atmosphere.

We were up against a team from Torrance and

they had this guy Bart Johnson, who had been named high school basketball player of the year in Southern California, pitching against us. He was a big kid, six-foot-five, known as Black Bart, who would go on to pitch for the Chicago White Sox. He was shutting us down, protecting a 1–0 lead late in the game when he walked two guys in front of me. I lived for opportunities like that. I doubled down the line, the only hit we got off him, and that scored both runners and put us up 2–1. We were one out away from winning the game and got an infield popup, just what we needed. It drifted in front of home plate, a routine play for our catcher, a great athlete named Lynn Mason who was tough as nails and a first-rate linebacker on the football team. But Lynn lost the ball in the sun. The runners advanced and on the next pitch, a guy got a hit and we lost 3–2. We were that close to the state championship. Lynn went right in and tore a sink off the wall, he was so strong — and so ticked off.

The Braves were in Atlanta finishing up a homestand with three games against the Giants and then were due to fly to L.A. for a weekend series against the Dodgers. The Braves had upped my bonus nine times by then. They were getting my attention. Bill

White, the Braves' area scout, kept coming to the house to talk to my mother, who was negotiating for me. My dad would do his best to stop by when White was there and run him off. But he kept coming back, making the case to my mama that it was in my best interests to sign with the Braves. The team offered to fly my mother and me down to L.A. on Friday, August 18, so I could practice with the team and they could get a look at me. Up until then, the organization was trusting the word of Bill White. Braves General Manager Paul Richards, who had signed Joe Morgan and Mike Cuellar when he was GM of the Houston Colt .45s, would be there in L.A., so he'd be able to watch me, too.

My mother and I talked it over and decided to take that trip and make up our minds down there in Los Angeles. My father was 100 percent opposed. A year earlier that would have been enough to stop me in my tracks. But now I had responsibilities. Now I had to make my own decisions. What I needed was guidance.

Carroll Williams of Santa Clara was a good man and I felt like he was giving it to me straight. He'd driven up to Yountville and watched us narrowly lose that game to Torrance. We talked over my choice.

His advice: "If you get a large bonus, you should sign. If not, you should come to college." The Braves' first offer had been down around $6,000 and he didn't know they were going to up their offer to more than $30,000.

Williams had tried to persuade the Santa Clara baseball coach, Sal Taormina, to come up with him and get another look at me. But apparently Taormina wasn't interested based on what he'd seen when I visited the campus. Williams talked up my athletic potential to Taormina, but he'd been dismissive. I never was much of a tryout player. I could run, but I was skinny.

"He's OK," Taormina said. "He needs a little seasoning. He doesn't go back on the ball well."

Coach McCullough was never one to tell me what to do, or even telegraph what he thought I should do, but looking back this is how he remembers it, and keep in mind, I was only about five-foot-nine as a high school junior and didn't reach six feet until after I graduated. "You weren't really tall enough to go real far in basketball beyond being a good college player," he says now. "You grew up a baseball guy and your dad was a baseball guy, so even though basketball was your favorite sport, I figured baseball would be your thing eventually."

I guess he knew something I didn't. It was deadline time all around — deadline to accept my scholarship to Santa Clara or not, deadline to sign with the Braves or not. My mom and I flew down to Los Angeles and that was the first time I had the privilege to meet Hank Aaron. He prefers "Henry," but I always called him Hammer, as in Hammerin' Hank, or sometimes just Ham for short. My mother wasn't a big baseball fan, but she knew who Hank Aaron was. Everybody knew who Willie Mays and Hank Aaron were. The previous Wednesday back in Atlanta, Hammer hit his thirtieth home run of the season in a game against the Giants, meaning that for ten of the previous eleven seasons he'd hit thirty or more homers. He had great wrists and a beautiful swing and he was Mr. Consistency. My mama knew he was a great player and she saw he was also a good man, a sensitive and intelligent man, mentally strong. He reminded me of somewhere between my dad and my uncles. So she asked Hank to look out for me, and he said he would. To this day he has fulfilled that promise.

They put us up at the team hotel and I rode on the bus to go work out with the team before the game. I met Joe Torre. I met Felipe Alou, who gave me one of his bats — which my mom saved and gave to me years later when Felipe was managing the Giants, and I had him sign it. I was a Dodgers fan and my hero on the team was Tommy Davis, a batting champion in '62 and '63, so I was thrilled to go to Dodger Stadium with the Braves. I was even more thrilled when they suited me up and I went out and took batting practice. There I was, looking about fifteen years old, and they'd given me a uniform with no name on the back so some of the fans there for BP were kind of giving it to me.

"Hey, no-number!" one called out.

"That guy doesn't even have a number," someone else yelled and they all laughed.

On the bus ride back to the hotel I sat next to Hank Aaron. My mother had asked him to keep an eye on me, after all. It wasn't like we were just shooting the breeze. How much does a kid talk to Hank Aaron? But he talked to me about the choice I had to make about signing with the Braves or going to college. He asked some questions about me and about our family. He thought it over. He gave me a long look. Then he gave me the advice not of a concerned coach, but of a fellow ballplayer.

"If you have enough confidence to be in the big leagues by the time your college class graduates, then go ahead and sign," he told me. "If not, then you go to school."

Confidence? That was something I had. I knew that if I signed and joined the Braves organization, I'd hit the big leagues way before my college class would graduate four years later. I knew because I was going to make sure that happened, no matter what it took. I knew I had athletic talent, which was why they wanted me. I could run. I was quick. I could jump. I could hit and I could throw. And I felt I was smart enough to outthink most of them, too. But I had to develop more strength. I'd need to work at it to get better at baseball, but I'd grown up thinking of hard work as a given. That came naturally to me. Sure, part of me would have loved to spend my time hanging around in some crash pad in the Haight, sleeping until noon and living for music and meeting girls. But I could never have shrugged off my responsibilities like that. To me those responsibilities were very real. If I hadn't been raised the way I was, if I hadn't been taught to be responsible, then I could have jumped off the deep end a whole bunch of ways.

Putting on a Braves uniform and taking the field with Hank Aaron and the others had moved me a long way toward being ready to decide finally, but there was nothing easy about it. That night in our room in the Braves' team hotel in L.A. I prayed on it before I went to bed. I was direct in my prayers, as I often was. See, back before the draft I'd prayed to be chosen by anyone but the Braves, because the South in those years was the last place I wanted to be. I prayed more and said: You ignored my last prayer, so maybe this time you can listen. I prayed to wake up the next morning with a sense of clarity and you know what? That prayer was answered. Waking up the next day I knew what I needed to do.

My mother and I went up to the suite of Paul Richards, the Braves' GM, to talk over my plans. That was some big suite. Richards went in to take a shower and left my mother and me sitting there watching his TV, and I started looking around the room. There on top of the TV he'd left a big wad of money wrapped up in a rubber band. It was such a big wad of cash it needed a rubber band to hold it all together! For all I knew those were ones, but it looked like a lot of money to me. Paul Richards was no fool. He knew that would get my attention.

I decided to sign, and my mom signed, too.
I promised my mom I'd go to college anyway, I'd
find a way to do both, and I did. We flew home to
Sacramento and I enrolled at American River College
for that whole academic year and then right away
they sent me down to Austin, Texas, to get my feet
wet. That time of year, the only option was to send
me to Double-A, even if I might be in over my head,
and that's what they did. My head was spinning.
One day I'm playing in front of all my friends for
the American Legion championship of California,
then I'm in L.A. taking batting practice at Dodger
Stadium, then I'm in Texas, an eighteen-year-old
kid among grown men. Luck goes a long way in life.
I was lucky to have Hank Aaron there to give me
advice and look out for me, and I was lucky to have
some great teammates in Austin.

That was where I met Ralph Garr, who is my
best friend in baseball to this day. He was in the
same draft as I was, but he was coming out of
Grambling State University and I was out of high
school. Cito Gaston was on that team, too. I'll never forget, my first game of pro ball was facing the
Arkansas Travelers at Ray Winder Field in Little
Rock, Arkansas, in a state that for years was the

third-most segregated in the country behind only Mississippi and Alabama.

So there I was in the Double-A Texas League, down in Little Rock in 1967, playing the outfield with Cito and Ralph, and I was hearing some strange things from the crowd already. A ball was hit to me — the first ball hit to me in my professional career — and I dropped it! That crowd was on me! They called me some names I'd never heard before and I started crying. I found out later that Ray Winder Field was near a mental hospital, and they brought a whole group over and sat them down behind me in right field. They were the only fans out there, and they were the ones yelling all this deeply racist stuff I had never heard before. But I didn't know that at the time. This was a brave new world for me, nothing like growing up in California. This was the South. Cito said he'd take care of me and he did, too. That was the only error I made those two weeks I played with Austin. I didn't want to go through all that again. I only played in nine games, and had a .231 average, but it was a taste of the action.

I came home and started that academic year, which would run through June 1968. I took a full load, fifteen units, because I'd promised my mother

I'd graduate — and also because if you weren't taking fifteen units you were eligible for the draft and might be sent over to Vietnam! My mother went back to school, too, so she and I were actually college students at the same time. Soon my brother Robert and my sister were in college, too. That was an economic mess, potentially, way more financial strain than the family could handle. But I helped pay for my mother and my brothers and sisters to go to college by signing with the Braves.

I knew my father was going to be angry with me for signing. I didn't know he'd sue me. Really I shouldn't have been too surprised. He was always a very determined individual, and he believed that signing a professional baseball contract was the wrong move for me. In doing that I was forfeiting the right ever to earn a college scholarship for basketball or football. And what if the baseball didn't work out? He had told me where he stood. I defied his wishes anyway — and had to pay a price. I felt like I was a man now, free to make adult decisions, and I make one and my father pulls me into a courtroom. Can you imagine? There we were, my dad on one side of the court room with his lawyer and over on the other side my mother and me and our lawyer.

When the smoke had cleared it was a mixed kind of verdict: My dad couldn't nullify my signing with the Braves, because of the Coogan Act, named for child actor Jackie Coogan, but it was determined that the state of California would be a trustee of my financial affairs until I turned twenty-one. I could take some of my signing bonus and buy my first car, a canary yellow 1968 Oldsmobile 442 with spoked rims, and use some to help the family, but most would be kept in a fund overseen by the state and invested in IBM and Standard Oil of California stock. I thought that at age eighteen I was grown enough to make up my own mind, but back then twenty-one was the age that mattered. I was hot and didn't cool down for a long time. I didn't speak to my dad for three years.

Chapter 6

My Education Continues

I was at American River College from September 1967 to June 1968. That was a confusing but beautiful period for me all at the same time — the Vietnam War, the Black Power movement, hippies, free love, baseball, church and above all a music scene that was exploding all around. We might go into Davis to see music or all the way into San Francisco, if we could. I always loved that drive. When you crossed over the Bay Bridge, checking out that view of Alcatraz and beyond, then you came sliding down toward the city by the bay, man, that always felt good. You didn't know what the night held, but you knew it was going to be some kind of adventure.

Sometimes the music came to us. Since Monterey the previous June I'd been talking about

Hendrix with anyone I thought was cool, and now in February 1968 he was coming to California again. Hendrix had been touring Europe, but these would be his first shows in the United States since the previous August. In January he'd started recording tracks for the album *Are You Experienced,* including his version of Dylan's "All Along the Watchtower," which would help make that album his first No. 1 hit in the U.S. when it came out later that year. The tour started with a series of dates in San Francisco at the Winterland Ballroom and Fillmore Auditorium and then on February 8 the Jimi Hendrix Experience came to the Sacramento State College men's gym for a concert organized by a group of Sac State students.

The second studio album from the Jimi Hendrix Experience, *Axis: Bold as Love,* had just come out and we got our hands on that and listened to it again and again. That just made us want to see Jimi live again that much more. The best cut on the new album had to be "Castles Made of Sand," which Jimi wrote. It's a heavy song, his way of sharing a little of what it was like for him growing up.

He cries "Oh girl, you must be mad

What happened to the sweet love you and
    me had?"
Against the door he leans and starts a scene,
And his tears fall and burn the garden green.
So castles made of sand, fall into the sea,
    eventually.

A *New York Times* reporter caught up with Jimi when he was in San Francisco for those shows and did a big piece. "Musically, he came up the black route, learning guitar to Muddy Waters records on his back porch, playing in Negro clubs in Nashville, begging his way onto Harlem bandstands, and touring for two years, lost in the bands of rhythm and blues headliners: the Isley Brothers, Joey Dee, Little Richard, and King Curtis. He even played the Fillmore once, but that was backing Ike and Tina Turner and long before the Haight-Ashbury scene," reporter Michael Lydon wrote.

I caught Ike and Tina Turner at Winterland, too, but that was later, in October 1970, when they were playing on a bill with an L.A. band called Spirit, known for their single "I Got a Line on You." Spirit was kind of psychedelic, very California, and they opened for Ike and Tina Turner? Why would you put those two acts together? I thought that was kind of weird.

I saw Jimi at Winterland in February 1968, too, just before Sacramento State. He didn't light anything on fire, but none of us cared. It was Jimi up there putting on a show and by then more and more people were catching on to this guy. The main detail of the show to remember was that along with some of their own songs, they mixed in a cover of the Beatles' "Sgt. Pepper's Lonely Hearts Club Band." Mitch Mitchell was banging away on the drums and you kind of thought it would be Sgt. Pepper's as Jimi laid down a guitar line, but you didn't really know until Jimi started singing, "It was twenty years ago..." and then went off on one of his short solos. That was cool, the nod to the Beatles, whose last concert together had been only a year and a half earlier at Candlestick Park in San Francisco.

The *New York Times* article that month went on to relay a story Hendrix told the reporter about his days playing backup to Little Richard. He and another of the musicians got tired of wearing the uniform given to them and went out and bought some sharp threads. A meeting was called by Little Richard himself. "I am Little Richard," he said. "I am the only one allowed to be pretty. Take off those shirts."

Jimi ended up in New York's Greenwich Village early in 1966, playing as Jimmy James, and took to the scene there. He played regular gigs at Cafe Wha?, met a lot of people, and was inspired to start writing his own songs.

"Dylan really turned me on — not the words or his guitar, but as a way to get myself together," Jimi told the *Times* reporter. "A cat like that can do it to you. Race, that was OK. In the Village, people were more friendly than in Harlem, where it's all cold and mean. Your own people hurt you more. Anyway, I had always wanted a more open and integrated sound. Top-40 stuff is all out of gospel, so they try to get everybody up and clapping, shouting 'Yeah, yeah.' We don't want to get everybody up. They should just sit there and dig it. And they must dig it, or we wouldn't be there."

True words, man, true words. People *were* digging it, no question. Looking back now, I also know what Jimi meant about the Village versus Harlem. The Village was like Haight-Ashbury at the time. I liked going to Harlem, but I liked going to the Village more, because I felt more at peace. Does that make sense? I was attracted to Harlem, but I felt I had to watch my back more in Harlem than I did in the Village. I've never seen hippies fighting. I didn't mind being around hippies. I didn't necessarily have to do what they did. But I didn't stand out. I moved from Riverside to the Sacramento area and I stood out everywhere. I couldn't even blend if I wanted to. But in the Village or Haight-Ashbury, Golden Gate Park, it was like I was invisible, and I liked that.

I had trouble most of my life, until about the eighth grade, fitting in or trying to fit in. I had funky shoes I wanted to get, or I had madras shirts and everyone was like, "What's wrong with you? Why are you so different? Why are you weird?" I heard them all. Then six months later I'd see them wearing the same stuff I'd been wearing before. So I said, "Am I weird? I know I'm different. Or am I ahead?" There was a time I didn't really fit in anywhere, like sixth grade and seventh grade and eighth grade. I didn't really fit in with the sons of brothers, and I didn't fit in with most of the white people. I tell my son now: You know something? It requires more strength to be different. You don't go out of your way. But you don't worry about being accepted. And if you've got the lead in life, you keep the lead. You just stay on that path wherever it's taking you. If they say you're "weird," who cares?

I talked some of my more conservative friends into going to see Jimi with me at Sacramento State in February 1968. The band came out and all around in the men's gym people were clapping like crazy even before they'd played a note, they were so excited to see Jimi Hendrix live. The first song was a cover of something called "Tax Free," and it started with a long spacey jam, a good minute or two of freewheeling psychedelic playing around before any words were sung, which I for one thought was cool, but my straight friends kept looking at me, like: *Are you serious? You expect me to get into this?* Sure enough, the song was one long instrumental. Next up was "Fire," as in "Let me stand next to your fire." That's also the song with the line "Aw move over, Rover, and let Jimi take over," which I've always liked. Next up were "The Wind Cries Mary" and "Hey Joe," both great Jimi songs, but I'd heard both at Monterey. Then came more of a surprise: Hendrix doing Dylan, like his "Like a Rolling Stone" at Monterey, was the best of both worlds, as far as I was concerned, and it took me awhile to realize Jimi was singing Dylan at Sacramento State.

He sits in your room, his tomb, with a fist full
   of tacks
Preoccupied with his vengeance
Cursing the dead that can't answer him back
I'm sure that he has no intention
Of looking your way, unless it's to say
That he needs you to test his inventions.

It was "Can You Please Crawl Out Your Window?" with the refrain "Use your arms and legs it won't ruin you." It wasn't a Dylan song I knew well, but it sure did sound like him and Jimi had a great time with it. He closed out his set with "Foxy Lady," another long instrumental, and then "Purple Haze." There was just no comparing Jimi with anyone else. He could do more with a guitar, he had a sense of play that pushed him always to try something new, and he looked like he was having so much fun, it rubbed off.

"There was no expectation of being pampered," Skip Maggiora, who was backstage handling the musical equipment that night, later told author Matt Taylor for an oral history of the concert. "He played to the crowd. The crowd loved him and I think he enjoyed the gig virtually as much. I remember them coming off the stage really excited. The three of them felt like they had played one of their better performances."

That same month my Atlanta Braves teammates were reporting for spring training in Florida. I could picture them out there, stretching and taking BP, Hank Aaron and Felipe Alou and Ralph Garr. I wouldn't be joining them. I was a college student. I wouldn't be leaving to start playing in the Braves organization again until that June, but it wasn't like I was taking it easy. That was not a luxury I had. Too much was at stake. I had to make it, man, because I didn't want my dad to be right. We hadn't spoken in months at that point after I signed without his permission. If I was a washout, he'd be able to say "I told you so." I wasn't going to let that happen.

I developed my own training regimen, and it was a good one, too. I always liked swimming and I decided I'd swim most every day. I'd do a baseball workout every day, of course. But I also had the idea that it would be smart to take my most obvious asset as a player at that point, my speed and quickness, and improve on that. So I went to talk to the track coach at American River College, Al Baeta, to see if he might work with me, even though I wasn't on the team — and couldn't be, since I'd signed a professional baseball contract.

"I want to get in shape," I told Coach Baeta. "Can you help me?"

He said he'd be glad to give it a try. He could see I was serious, but I could also see he was curious how committed I would really be. It didn't take long for him to see that I meant it when I said I wanted to work.

"You're naturally drawn to young people who want to improve themselves and as a result you're very willing to help them," Coach Baeta says now, looking back.

He's a great coach who went on to a long career, and he's been inducted into the Sacramento Running Association Hall of Fame.

"You came down to the track and we developed a program for you," Baeta says now. "You really blossomed in the program, both in terms of your fitness and your excitement about the program. We did work on mechanics, nothing major, but a thing or two. You were naturally a sound mechanical runner and adapted to things extremely well. You would do anything I asked you to do."

I figured we'd just focus on sprints, but Coach

had more in mind than that. He taught me that for a sprinter, recovery work was every bit as important as speed work. We did a lot of interval work. I'd run fifty or sixty yards hard, then walk the same distance, and we'd up the distance to three hundred and beyond. We didn't do any weights. I didn't ask for that and Coach didn't suggest it. Those were different days in terms of how much weight training track athletes do. You check out the World Championships now and the top sprinters look like trucks. But Coach did emphasize stretching to enhance my flexibility, and I was a little impatient with that at first, but over the years that really paid dividends for me. It might have even helped keep me healthy. One stat from my big-league career that jumps out at a lot of people is this: I had nineteen seasons in the majors, and played in 2,039 games, and never once went on the disabled list. I'm proud of that one.

I'd like to thank Coach Baeta for helping me build the foundation to do that. I did my best to thank him at the time, but I want him to know all these years later I haven't forgotten how much he helped me. "You were just a kid when you came to me," Coach says now. "You were quite evidently very, very competitive, but you were very respectful of everyone.

You were very appreciative that I would take the time, given that you were not on my team, but it was really my pleasure."

I was eager to start swinging the bat again in games that mattered. I'd be joining Atlanta's Class A affiliate in the Western Carolinas League, the Greenwood Braves, who played their games at Legion Stadium in Greenwood, South Carolina. It was good I'd prepared myself physically as well as I could, because I don't know if you can ever prepare yourself mentally for as jarring a transition as what I went through leaving the cool, hip, Jimi Hendrix-loving world of Northern California in late June 1968 and landing in South Carolina. It was maybe 2,500 miles in the air, but that did not begin to explain the distance you traveled. If you were African-American, it felt like traveling back in time. Wow. I had never seen segregation and here it was in full force. All I ever asked of anyone was treat me like a man, give me a chance to be who I am and you can be who you are, but to a lot of people in the South at that time, all they saw was the color of my skin. To this day, it's hard for me to watch a movie like *Selma*. I can't just sit there and watch it as entertainment. For me it's all too real. It starts bringing back memories of things I really don't want to remember.

I'd done the work back home in California to give myself every chance to succeed, but now it was time to get it done. I had a big job to do in proving my father wrong. My first game that year was at home on June 27, 1968, against the visiting Salisbury Senators. They had me leading off and playing left field and I missed the cycle by a homer — I tripled, doubled and singled and scored four times. The next day I had two more hits. As the *Index-Journal* newspaper in Greenwood put it, "Dusty Baker, the Braves' new outfielder, continued his spree at the plate with a double and a single." I was hitting the ball, had my average up at .374, and my speed was making a mark: "Dusty Baker had singled, stole second and raced to third as the catcher's throw knocked his helmet off and the ball bounced into left field," the *Index-Journal* reported.

I batted .342 for Greenwood in fifty-two games, with three triples and six home runs, and earned a September call-up. I'd had no spring training, hadn't swung a bat against live pitching until June 27 and now at age nineteen I was going to the big leagues. I'd have loved to call my father to tell him, but we weren't on speaking terms, so I called my mama and she was so happy. It was good to see the guys again, especially Hank Aaron, who had not forgotten his pledge to my mother to look out for me. He gave me as much good advice as anyone in my life. I remember four years later when we were going up against Bob Gibson he told me: "Don't dig in against Bob Gibson. He'll knock you down. He'd knock down his own grandmother if she dared to challenge him. Don't stare at him. Don't smile at him. Don't talk to him. He doesn't like it. If you happen to hit a home run, don't run too slow, don't run too fast. If you happen to want to celebrate, get in the tunnel first. And if he hits you, don't charge the mound, because he's a Golden Gloves boxer."

Back then a young kid did not get thrown straight into the thick of the action. I made my major-league debut on September 7, when my manager Lum Harris had me pinch-hit for pitcher Phil Niekro in the seventh inning of a home game against the Astros, and I grounded out to shortstop. Three days later, still in Atlanta, we were facing Bobby Bonds and the Giants and I pinch-hit again, this time for catcher Walt Hriniak, and struck out. On September 14 at Dodger Stadium they used me as a pinch-runner, so at least I got into the game, but nowhere near home plate.

The Braves had made an unusual move in August. They signed Leroy Robert Paige, known to everyone as Satchel Paige, one of the greatest pitchers in the history of baseball, as a player/coach. The twist was: Satchel by then was sixty-two years old. As one headline put it: *ANCIENT SATCHEL PAIGE SIGNED TO BRAVE PACT,* adding the subhead *Famed Athlete to Advise, May Pitch Part-time.* The accompanying article (a UPI report in the Cumberland, Maryland, *News*) explained, "Paige, still without any trace of gray in his hair, told a news conference that he could pass good advice on to Braves pitchers. But he said he wasn't sure about his pitching abilities. 'I'll just have to go out and see if I can unfold,' he said.... Paige last pitched in the majors in 1965 when he hurled three innings of scoreless ball for Kansas City against Boston. Since then he has been a deputy sheriff, and has worked in only a few exhibitions."

Braves executive Bill Bartholomay made the move in part to remedy a wrong: Satchel was a star in the Negro Leagues, both an amazing pitcher with one of the best fastballs ever and a fun-loving showman, who used to like to have his infielders sit down and then strike out the side. Through the best years of his career he was never allowed to pitch in the big leagues, held back by the same bigotry that kept all blacks out until Jackie came along. Satchel finally made his big-league debut in 1948, a forty-two-year-old rookie, and went 6–1 for Cleveland that year. He pitched in parts of six seasons in the majors, but because he'd been held back for so long, he fell short of earning enough big-league service time to qualify for a pension. That was the injustice Bartholomay and the Braves sought to address.

It was a standup move, and Bill and I later became friends, so I'll let him explain for himself how it went down: "I was thinking that Leroy, which was what I called him, was approximately a month short of qualifying for the Major League Baseball players pension and that was because of the politics and the fact that as an African-American he did not receive any credit for all the years he played baseball but not in the American or National League. His agent reached out to all the major-league teams, including the Braves, and asked if there would be any interest in employing Satch. Apparently I was the only one that responded favorably to that, and we were glad to have him with us. Leroy was a fantastic guy. We loved him. He had a repertoire of pitches like no other pitcher I had ever had, and he had about five windups, including his famous windmill one. If there had been a popularity contest in our clubhouse, he'd have won it hands down."

Back then, as rookies you were expected to caddy for the veterans, which amounted to doing just about everything for them. I caddied for Satch. Hard to believe, but there I was, a nineteen-year-old kid, hanging around with Satch all the time. He'd call me "Daffy." I told him, "My name is Dusty." He said, "Daffy, I know what your name is." I'd have to haul his bags from the bus up to his hotel room. I'd carry all his fishing rods, because he liked to travel with all that. People would constantly be giving him stuff, so I'd carry that as well, or Ralph Garr and I both would, since he caddied for Satch, too. But the carrying was the least of it. Most of all I listened. I soaked up whatever I could from Satch. One week with Satch was more of an education than a year of university. He said things like "Don't eat fried food, it angries up the blood." And "Age is a question of mind over matter. If you don't mind, it doesn't matter." And "Work like you don't need the money. Love like you've never been hurt. Dance like nobody's watching."

We headed to Houston for a series at the Astrodome. On September 17 I pinch-hit for our pitcher and had my first base hit in the big leagues, a swinging bunt against Mike Cuellar, a Cuban who would go on to win 185 games in the big leagues. From Houston we flew to San Francisco and for me it couldn't have been much better. I was a big-leaguer now, at least for the time being, and I'd be flying out with the Braves to the city where I'd been hanging out in the Haight-Ashbury district whenever I could. As much as the news media and the youth culture were focused on what was happening with the San Francisco sound and with Flower Power and the hippies, Vietnam War protests and the Panthers, the Giants also had a lot going on. They still had Willie Mays and Willie McCovey batting three-four, one of the all-time greatest tandems, and starting pitchers Juan Marichal and Gaylord Perry.

This was my first game playing in front of all my homeboys from Sacramento and my mom and all my relatives. I really missed my dad. Knowing him, he was probably there in the stadium somewhere, but since I didn't invite him and we weren't in contact,

I was never going to know. Our first game in the series, my buddy Ralph Garr pinch-hit and then I was sent in for him as a defensive replacement to play center field. My spot in the order came around and I had to face Marichal, who was already 25–8 at that point in the season. Not many pitchers got under my skin, but as a nineteen-year-old kid facing the great Juan Marichal, of course I was nervous. I hit a little dribbler and was so jacked up, I flew down the line and beat it out for a hit. You should have seen me on first base. I was not going to show up Marichal and act too pleased with myself. It was a little dribbler! But inside I was not about to miss the chance to enjoy this.

Carroll Williams, the Santa Clara University basketball coach, was listening to the game on the radio and heard my at-bat. Dusty Baker? Already in the big leagues? He called the SCU baseball coach, Sal Taormina, who'd said he had no interest in me.

"You remember that kid Dusty Baker I was trying to get you to take another look at a year ago?" Williams needled him. "The one you said was 'OK'? He's with the Atlanta Braves now. He just got a hit against Juan Marichal."

Two days later I came into the third game of the

series to play center field as a defensive replacement, once again, and had one more at-bat: I grounded out to shortstop, and that was my season with the Braves. All in all I was satisfied. I had no choice but to succeed. There was no way I was going to give my dad any openings to tell me he was right. I'd put together a strong season at A ball, gotten a cup of coffee at the big-league level, and I'd had the chance to be around amazing figures like Satchel Paige and Henry Aaron.

I went back home to Sacramento for the offseason ready to hang with my friends and talk over my September in the big leagues, and I was in luck: The Jimi Hendrix Experience was coming back to San Francisco for three nights at the Winterland Ballroom starting on October 11. Dennis and I drove in with some other friends and found a cheap motel in North Beach, right around the corner from the Condor Club, where Carol Doda became probably the most famous stripper in the country. We weren't allowed in Carol Doda's. We were too young. We went up to our hotel room and flipped a coin to see who would get to sleep on mattresses, which we pulled off the box springs and threw on the floor, and who would sleep on the box springs. We didn't care where we slept. We were in the city to have a good time. The pact I'd had with my buddies never to smoke was something we took very seriously, and we stuck to it totally — for a long time. But by this point, we were starting to smoke a little weed. It was 1968, after all. We headed downstairs from our hotel and were walking around when we saw a couple of guys across the street smoking a joint.

"Hey, man, that guy looks like Jimi Hendrix," Dennis said.

We laughed. But then we looked closer and the guy really did look like Jimi Hendrix. We got closer and we saw it *was* Jimi Hendrix. I couldn't believe it. I knew every word of every song Jimi did and here he was, right in front of us.

"Let's ask him if he wants to try some of what we got," one of my friends said, and we all laughed again, but we figured: Why not?

I was designated to go over and talk to them, and after I broke the ice and we were standing there against the wall smoking, the other dudes came over. That's right: My claim to fame is I smoked a joint with Jimi Hendrix.

Chapter 7

Learning the Meaning of Friendship

'd played well enough in 1968 that the Braves were excited about my potential. If I could hit better than .340 in Single A after no spring training and no game action in May, what could I do if I arrived in camp just like everyone else? I told them I was planning on going to college again and they told me: *No, no, no, you're on the fast course now. We need you at spring training.* I was getting used to disappointing people. I'd disappointed my father the year before when I signed with the Braves. I'd disappointed the coach from Santa Clara, Carroll Williams, who always treated me right, when I told him that in the end I wasn't coming to play for him, even though I'd signed a letter of intent. And I disappointed my mother when I told her the Braves insisted I go to spring training in '69. I was looking forward to a full year of baseball, wanting to build on what I'd done so far, but I also had the Vietnam War to worry about.

That was a heavy time with the war in Southeast Asia. The Tet Offensive of early 1968 was the pivotal battle of the whole war. The protest movement hit another gear that year. President Lyndon B. Johnson decided not to seek reelection, knowing that he couldn't win with the war so unpopular. Friends of mine from school were over there fighting — and dying. I played football at Del Campo with a guy named Denny Showers. He was sent to Vietnam in the infantry and on March 25, 1968, his unit was in Quang Tri Province, along the central coast north of Da Nang, when the action got heavy and he was killed. "Multiple fragmentation wounds," according to the official military notice. It was hard for me to imagine my friend Denny from high school football lying face down in the jungle over there.

The Braves suggested that like many in my era, I enlist in the military reserves so I could further my career without taking the risk of being drafted. My first thought was to enlist in the Air Force Reserve, because I wanted something easy, but a lot of other people had the same idea, and the Air Force Reserve filled up first. My next option would have been the Navy Reserve, but they wanted a four-year commitment. It came down to a choice between the Marines and the National Guard and that was no choice at all as far as I was concerned: There was no way I was joining the National Guard. They were being called out on riot duty. I might have to shoot some hippie protester or help squash an anti-war protest or race riot. I'd be considered a Benedict Arnold. That was not for me.

I joined the Marines and in the end I have to say it was good for me at the time. It taught me teamwork. All these things that happened to me — joining the Braves, going to the South, meeting Hank Aaron, seeing a different outlook on life at such a young age — it all confused me, but it also helped me in the long run. They sent us to training at Parris Island, South Carolina, and Camp Lejeune, North Carolina, in 1969 and I remember on the first day they announced that out of all of us, one would be chosen as honor man and that would mean he'd be decked out in dress blue on graduation day and everyone else was going to be in green. I was thinking to myself: *You might as well just give that to me right now and save all this time!* I'd been hunting all my life and could shoot a rifle with the best of them. I was fast and I was fit. Above all I was competitive. And sure enough, I was the honor man and I wore dress blue.

The thing about being in the Marine Corps Reserve is you serve your time here and there, so each time you might end up in a different unit with totally different duties. I had to do a summer camp every year, missing two weeks of ball, and one weekend every month. I spent some time in a 50-caliber howitzer unit. I was in a transportation unit in Atlanta. Then I wound up in an MP unit — you know, military police — which is a riot control unit for the military. That was just what I wanted to avoid and that's what I was stuck doing. The unit was sent from Shreveport, Louisiana, to Camp Pendleton in Southern California and I was serving my required time with them and they put me on brig detail. That was heavy duty. These were guys accused of war crimes who were being held to go to Leavenworth Penitentiary. You were under orders not even to speak to any of these prisoners, so I was doing my best to keep my mouth shut, never an easy thing for me, up in the tower with a shotgun and search lights. If you saw them trying to escape, you were supposed to fire a warning shot and yell out "Halt!"

"Dusty!" someone said in a loud whisper.

I didn't even want to look to see who was calling my name. But I glanced down and saw that it was Levi Guinn, one of the smartest guys that I grew up with in Riverside. He was two or three years older than me and way ahead in a lot of ways. I couldn't believe he was in the brig.

"What are you doing here, man?" I asked him.

"Dude, I was in Vietnam," he said. "I was supposed to shake a bush to draw enemy fire. I refused to do it."

I walked away to try to get my thoughts together and just kept shaking my head. Finally I reached down to my shotgun and took out the shells. There was no way I was going to shoot Levi Guinn, whether he was telling the truth about what happened or not. There was no way I was going to shoot any of them locked up there. I came back the next day, and sure enough, it happened again.

"Dusty!" a voice called out.

It was Melvin Baxter, the class clown back in Riverside. Again I walked away shaking my head. That really got to me. If something had gone down before either of those guys called out to me, I might have ended up shooting my homeboys who I grew up with in Riverside. That shook me up. Here I was, twenty years old, and going through some heavy stuff. I tell people that was a great time to be that age, but also a very tumultuous and confusing time. Everybody was hollering about freedom back then, you know what I mean? You didn't know what to think or how to be, but you did know that it was our time. I didn't know how lucky I was to have been in that era. Two things kept me straight: the fact my parents had raised me in the church and raised me to be responsible as the oldest of five, and the good friendships I had to keep my head screwed on right.

One of the new faces around the Braves starting in 1969 was Orlando Cepeda, a future Hall of Famer who already had eleven big-league seasons under his belt by then. He hit forty-six homers and had 142 RBIs for the 1961 Giants, just missing out on Most Valuable Player, and was league MVP in '67 when he had 111 RBIs for the Cardinals. When I met him at spring training in Florida he and I connected right away, above all through music. I told him all about Jimi Hendrix and would play songs for him and he would nod and listen, but for him as a fan of jazz it was something very different. We'd be out on the field and he'd wave me over and have me sing Jimi Hendrix tunes for some of his Latin friends on other teams. They made me like a little clown, and I didn't mind at all.

"Go, John! Go, John! Go, John!" Orlando would call out, laughing, as I sang "Purple Haze" or "Crosstown Traffic."

I loved hanging around with Orlando, and later I played on his winter ball team in Puerto Rico, which was where he was from. Orlando turned me on to all kinds of jazz, from Latin stuff like Eddie Palmieri to Stanley Turrentine, the jazz saxophonist known as "The Sugar Man," to Brother Jack McDuff, the organist and band leader, to music I probably should have known already but didn't, like the Crusaders and Quincy Jones. It was my friendship with Orlando that really sent me to another level of connection with music. We listened to Thelonious Monk together, and John Coltrane and Chick Corea. He taught me a different sound to listen to and a different way of listening.

In those years Carlos Santana was the opening act at dozens of shows we saw in San Francisco, so when Orlando asked me about Santana I had that one covered. "Santana?" I said. "I must have seen him fifty times." Then I was down in Puerto Rico playing winter ball in late 1971 and saw Santana perform at Hiram Bithorn Stadium, the big baseball park in San Juan, the capital. Here he was, playing for a huge crowd of Latins who understood and loved his music. It was Halloween and the vibe was far more electric than anything I'd experienced with Santana in California. That stayed with me. In those years I was going to Mexico, Puerto Rico and Venezuela playing winter ball and listening to salsa and meringue and all kinds of other styles. I was fortunate my mother had made me learn to speak Spanish, so I understood. The only two black artists they knew down there were James Brown and Gladys Knight and they'd always ask me about them. Back then no one had heard much Brazilian music, but one time in Caracas, Venezuela, my friend Iran Paz, who I'd played with on the Greenwood Braves, took me to see a concert by the Brazilian Eumir Deodato and he put on a show all right, with a high-energy performance that was somewhere between Latin jazz and rock.

There was a music revolution going on big-time. The races were starting to interchange the music. I'd grown up with black music, from the blues to gospel, and moving to Northern California when I did my timing was great to tune into the San Francisco sound. That all came together at Monterey. Now in the South I was going to see concerts ever week, either at the Fox or the Omni or Underground Atlanta, and taking my education further. I was listening to Gladys Knight and Bobby Womack and Little Johnny Taylor and Isaac Hayes and Al Green and Clarence "Slip Away" Carter. I was into the Temptations. One of my favorites was the Impressions with Curtis Mayfield, like "People Get Ready." I got into Patti LaBelle, who made a splash later with "Lady Marmalade" (You know, all that *Voulez-vous coucher* stuff?).

I was in for a little bit of a letdown when it came to baseball. I'd gone from A ball to the big leagues as a September call-up in '68 and so far as the organization was concerned, I still needed seasoning in the minor leagues. I was the youngest on every team then. I was always called the kid. I played mostly for Double-A Shreveport in '69, but earned a promotion to Triple-A Richmond in the International League and then in September went hitless in my seven at-bats with the big-league Braves. It took two more seasons playing mostly in Richmond before I finally was a full-time big-leaguer in 1972. I hit .321 that year with seventeen homers and 76 RBIs, and even showed up in the voting for league MVP, won that year by Johnny Bench. I went into that offseason knowing I had a job with the big-league club the next year. Then in '73 I finished with 99 RBIs and 101 runs scored.

I found that when you're a big-league ballplayer you're constantly meeting interesting people. It's up to you what you do when you meet them. I was always with Hank, and the closer he got to Babe Ruth's career home-run record, the more excitement there was. All the black leaders of the South wanted to meet him. I remember meeting Maynard Jackson with Hank before Maynard was elected the first African-American mayor of Atlanta, and those were never handshake meetings, we all did some talking. When we were in Chicago, we went over to Jesse Jackson's house and Billy Preston was there, so all I wanted to do was talk music with Billy Preston, you know, like "Nothing From Nothing," but the conversation was wide ranging. We met Andrew Young, who was elected to Congress from Georgia in 1972. The governor of Georgia at that time was a former peanut farmer named Jimmy

Carter, and I got to know him through Hank as well. In fact, Ralph Garr and I would drop by the State Capitol to see the governor and his mother, Mama Lillian. His office was near the stadium, less than a mile away, so we'd often stop in before a game, and we might talk baseball or we might talk about the South. The governor liked to eat lunch in his office as he worked, so sometimes we'd have a sandwich with him.

Through every one of those meetings I learned more and gained perspective. I gained a truer outlook on life and race relations through all those experiences. My mom was in school then, majoring in black studies, and eventually she taught at Sacramento City College, and that experience in the South helped teach me that all black dudes weren't good and all white people with an accent weren't necessarily bad. Some of my closest friends now were people I met in the South. I was there from the age of nineteen to twenty-seven and after that I was ready to come home to California and I was ready to win. They traded me to the Dodgers before the 1976 season, and I soon got a taste of winning there, as the Dodgers took a couple of pennants in the late '70s and then beat the Yankees in the 1981 World Series.

I was sure I'd always be in regular contact with the people I was close to back in Riverside and Sacramento, but that was getting tougher. The good news was my father and I did reconcile. I turned twenty-one and the state of California was no longer a trustee of my finances. I was in control of my money now. I looked at the value of the stock in my name for IBM and Standard Oil of California and noticed that a funny thing had happened: The value of those stocks had roughly tripled in the three years since I'd received my signing bonus from the Braves. It had been a very shrewd investment. My father had not been trying to hurt me, he'd been trying to help me. He was trying to save me from myself. I told him as much and we put it all behind us and were close from then on. I learned valuable lessons about money from that strange experience, and have always tried to apply them ever since. Make good decisions, be careful, and don't bet your future on a whim.

I'd thought I'd stay tight with my old group of friends, great buddies who had shared the experience of hitting a J with Jimi Hendrix. My best friend of all was Dennis Kludt. He'd lost his parents and my whole family had always treated him like one of our own. My parents liked him and welcomed him over to the house any time he wanted to come over. But in the early '70s something started to change. All that time in the South did some work on my head. I felt myself a changed man. I was thrust into many environments in a short period of time that really jarred me and made me question many of the assumptions of my earlier years. My experiences in the South made me look back at high school and see some things in a new light. There were flashes of racism I was willing to overlook at the time and in retrospect I regretted that. Too much that I saw and experienced firsthand in the South was flat-out unacceptable to me and I knew we had to have change, major change, in this country. I wasn't sure if I could continue to have white people as close friends.

I thought Dennis and I were going to be on different sides of the revolution. So I quit writing to him, and quit calling.

It was kind of weird for me, I'll admit. Dennis and I talked at least once a month or so going all the way back to my first year in Sacramento when we played baseball together on the Del Campo team and became buddies. Now in early 1974 months had passed and we had not even spoken. I was in Florida for another spring training, looking forward to a good year, hanging with good friends like Ralph Garr, playing cards at home every night. I was driving my blue 1974 Thunderbird after the Braves workout one day, stopped off in a shopping mall and was driving home afterwards when I had the strange sensation that someone was staring at me. I tried to ignore it and kept on driving, but I couldn't shake the sense that someone was watching me. I looked over at the car next to me and someone *was* staring at me: It was my old buddy Dennis Kludt, there in Florida.

He still laughs at the look on my face that day. I'll let him tell it: "I'm following you and staring at you. You didn't know what was going on. Then you looked over and recognized me and you about died!"

We both pulled over and had ourselves a good reunion. I was so surprised and so happy to see him, I didn't think about all that stuff that was cluttering up my head before. I just thought: It's Dennis.

The man had basically driven all the way across the country to see me. He and his wife, Yvonne, who I'd introduced him to, had gone on a long road trip in his white '68 Mustang, staying with friends along the way, and explored the country, all with the idea that they'd come to Florida so Dennis and I could talk face to face and clear the air — or not. Dennis and his wife were going to leave Florida that day, but they ended up staying another week and we had ourselves a good time. We'd stay up late playing cards, Dennis and me, Ralph Garr and Paul Casanova, our catcher from Cuba, and right after practice we'd go fishing. We could fish right out the back of our bungalow.

I remember calling my dad up that month and telling him about it. He always liked Dennis, but he heard me out. I was still trippin' on the black-white divide.

"He drove cross country to see you?" my dad asked.

"Uh-huh," I said.

"How many friends do you have, white or black, that would do that?" my dad asked me.

Chapter 8
Music Keeps Me Young

I was lucky enough to hang around Satchel Paige, who was full of personality in his sixties and didn't let himself be defined by age in any way. I've never much slowed down to think about it, but I guess that's how it is with me, too. I'm excited by too many things to feel that I need to change or stop being myself, even if I am moving in on my seventieth birthday. I guess it's all about loving what you love. If I'm into growing grapes, then I go all out and grow some great Syrah grapes and make excellent wine through Baker Family Wines. If I want to go hunting or fishing, I go all out and have a great time. Or even if I just want to hang out at home with my wife, Melissa, and our son Darren, who is nearing college age now, then *that's* what I'm doing all the way. But there's another part that might almost count as a secret: Deep down inside, I don't think of myself so much as a baseball man as I see myself as a music man, a blues man and much more than that. If the music is playing in your heart, you're always going to have a spring in your step and always going to be excited about life and about getting up in the morning, and you're always going to feel young. The first thing I do every morning is read my Bible and then I turn on the music. On the road I always had music. I had music on the team bus, and I had music in my hotel room. I used to call my music my roommate because after Ralph Garr I never had another roommate besides my music. My music is still my roommate and traveling partner all these years later.

If I could have been something other than a ballplayer, I'd have been an entertainer, a musician. One thing I've always liked about baseball and sports in general is that they break down racial barriers — there's no white or black or yellow in the batter's box — but music does that even more. I always felt that I could never really express myself as a ballplayer, no matter how I played, like I could as a musician. So I've been drawn to musicians and entertainers. But it goes the other way, too. A lot of musicians find themselves drawn to people in sports. Musicians revere athletes, and vice versa. You think about it, playing the blues, there's so much teamwork, so much camaraderie, so much communication without words between members of the band, it's a lot like how it is for athletes during a game. I think a lot of musicians like watching what we do as much as we like watching what they do. We're all in the public eye. We're all trying to get it right, since there are no do-overs in live music or baseball.

A lot of my good friends over the years have been entertainers. We connect right away. One of my longtime friends is Ronnie Laws, the saxophone player. He was from Houston and lived in L.A., so I got to know him in my years with the Dodgers. His dad wanted him to be a baseball player. Every time we went to Houston, which was three times a year, Ronnie's mom would cook us up a soul food lunch and it kept growing to where we had Kenny Landreaux, Pedro Guerrero, Lee Lacy, Reggie Smith, Bobby Welch, Derrel Thomas and Steve Howe. We'd need two cars. Ronnie or his mother would come pick us up and we'd go over there. Her other son was Hubert Laws, who played the flute, and her daughter

Debra sang. I wanted to talk music and she wanted to talk baseball.

I remember once when I was hanging out at a club in San Francisco listening to music, I looked over and saw I was sitting next to Carlos Santana. He was cool, man. He had his hat on and everything. I always liked Santana. We started talking and it was the most natural thing in the world. The thing about musicians, they hook up together in a minute, especially the blues guys. Guys show up out of nowhere and before you know it, they all start playing together, just jammin'.

Melissa and I used to go to John Handy's place up in the Fillmore in San Francisco, a nice little blues spot. I remember when the Fillmore itself reopened I went back there, where I'd seen Jimi Hendrix years earlier, and caught Tom Petty and the Heartbreakers. That's another one of my favorite guitarists, Tom Petty, and Bob Brenly met me for that show.

Sweetwater in Mill Valley was always a great spot to hit and I remember being there with Rusty Evans and Kenny Tennell, who I grew up with in Riverside, to see Rod Piazza, the guy who'd always been fiddling around with a harmonica when we were kids.

I remember nights at Sweetwater where you'd be lost in the music, hardly noticing who just walked in, but then you realized it was Bonnie Raitt or Clarence Clemons, just hanging out like you are. And then they might start jammin', too. It happened just like that one night when those two came in and we were talking. Everyone was having a good time. Later a young woman came up to me with a big smile.

"I love your music," she told me.

I just smiled at her and thanked her.

Someone asked me: "Did she really say that? Who did she think you were?"

I answered: "Doesn't matter, but I better move on, before she asks me to sing."

When I met John Lee Hooker that took it to another level for me. John Lee was born in Mississippi. His daddy was a sharecropper and a Baptist preacher. He played down-home Delta blues and no one did it better, as you know if you've heard his versions of "Crawling King Snake" and "One Bourbon, One Scotch, One Beer." He moved around a lot in his life, but spent a lot of time in California, especially as he got older. He was here so much that in 1997 he opened John Lee Hooker's Boom Boom Room in the Fillmore District. But John Lee and I go back further than that. I played for the Dodgers for eight seasons starting in 1976, and John Lee was a Dodgers fan. He had a house in Long Beach and would come to games. I signed a Dodgers uniform for him — and I found out later he had that framed and on the wall of one of his houses in the Bay Area.

I started managing the Giants in 1993 and that was a good year in a lot of ways: We won 103 games, but finished one game back of the Braves in the N.L. West and back then there was no wild card, so our season was over. I was named Manager of the Year, which was nice, but like I always tell people, and I say this in private or in public, doesn't matter to me: Baseball is all about the players, not the manager or anyone else. Matt Williams and Barry Bonds combined that year for eighty-four home runs and 233 RBIs. Bill Swift and John Burkett both won more than twenty games for us. We had good defense up the middle in Royce Clayton and Robby Thompson at short and second, and Darren Lewis in center field. And we had a lot of good character guys. I told Darren one time: *You're just how I'd want a son of mine to be.* And when I did have a son, I named him "Darren" after Darren Lewis.

If I was going to be a manager, San Francisco

was where I wanted to be back then. The city hadn't changed all that much at that point from how it was when I was a young kid hanging out in the Haight with my buddies. I still loved hanging out. Baseball can wear you out, mentally I mean, and San Francisco was always there to help you change the channel and just chill out. I was a regular at Slim's on Eleventh Street. Remember Boz Scaggs? That's a cool name. He was guitarist and lead singer for the Steve Miller Band and had a hit as a solo artist with "Lido Shuffle" in the late '70s. He opened Slim's in 1988 and tried to turn it into his dream night-club, and did a good job of it, too. Huey Lewis was there playing harmonica the night the club opened, and the word was out to musicians that this was a great venue. By the '90s when I started managing the Giants, it was the place to go. I saw Simply Red at Slim's, Bonnie Raitt, Funkadelic, Bootsy, Maceo Parker from the James Brown band — the list goes on and on.

So much was happening at Slim's, you felt part of the action even if you couldn't be there that night. Here are some of the highlights from those years, as recorded by Joel Selvin of the *San Francisco Chronicle*:

May 13, 1993

Under the name Dr. David Gunn, Pearl Jam plays a benefit. Eddie Vedder and Dave Grohl play catch with club dog Buster in the alley.

May 20, 1993

Green Day pays to replace onstage carpets it ruined.

July 11, 1993

With "Creep" on the radio, Radiohead sells out the band's first San Francisco appearance.

Oct. 21, 1993

No Doubt opens for the Dance Hall Crashers.

Nov. 9, 1993

On a two-night double bill with Lemonheads, Hole lead vocalist Courtney Love spends the weekend wandering around backstage in her slip, fighting over the phone with her husband, Kurt Cobain.

April 18, 1994

The first S.F. appearance by Beck, originally booked at out-of-the-way Olive Oyl's on the waterfront, moves to Slim's.

June 19, 1994

Sheryl Crow makes her first San Francisco appearance.

Aug. 13, 1995

First of three sold-out, ecstatic performances over the years by Dogstar, the famously bad rock band featuring Keanu Reeves. A bomb scare brings police to the club.

John Lee would sometimes come see me at Candlestick when I was manager of the Giants. He was a real baseball fan. At home he'd have three TV sets on at a time, each tuned to baseball, and he would pay close attention. He'd been a catcher way back when, and always loved to talk baseball with me. He came to a game as my guest in September 1995 and had himself so much fun, talking to the players in the clubhouse, wearing a fedora made of felt with diamond-and-gold pins shaped like musical notes. He watched the game from a broadcast booth, then came down afterward and we talked in my office for hours. My dad was there, and my youngest brother, Millard, from my dad's second marriage, who picked up a love of the blues from my dad, too. Deion Sanders played for the Giants that season and he was there in my office to hang with John Lee, too. Asked who his favorite Giants player was, John Lee said, "Royce Clayton." And why was that? "Because he's cool." Royce *was* cool. He had that right.

The next August, John Lee invited me to a big birthday party he was having. He was turning seventy-nine years old, but you'd never know it from talking to him. He was having himself so much fun all the time, he might as well have been a teenager. That was John Lee. He was still performing regularly, too. I went to that birthday party and met all kinds of people, including Elvin Bishop, whose guitar work I'd first seen at the Monterey Pop Festival in 1967. Elvin had actually seen John Lee's "Baker" Dodgers uniform and asked about me, and John Lee said he'd introduce us.

Elvin was my kind of guy. He's lived up in Marin County for years, and was actually born in California, but grew up in Iowa and Oklahoma. In

1960, he earned a National Merit Scholarship to attend the University of Chicago and study physics, and it was there in Chicago that he met Paul Butterfield and started playing guitar in his blues band. Elvin formed his own group before long and had a hit with "Fooled Around and Fell in Love" (he didn't sing on that one, though). Elvin has played with everyone you can think of. He played with Muddy Waters. He played with Lightnin' Hopkins. He and I could have talked music all night, or baseball, but instead we started talking fishing, which we're both serious about. After that we became fishing buddies.

"You know all the good spots," Elvin says. "You check it out and make sure it's going to be good. We always catch fish. But you're competitive. There are times when two guys will be out there using the same bait and one guy is catching all kinds of fish and the other can't catch anything. That's just part of fishing. But when it happens to you, your jaw gets tight. You don't like that!"

Elvin can kid me like that because we've had so many good times. One time I was with Elvin and Orlando Cepeda was there, too, and he took a look at Elvin and kind of did a double-take, and then he told him: "I know you! You were on one of Santana's records." Actually, it was some of Santana's guys who played on one of Elvin's records, but that was cool. Orlando saw everything from the Latin angle. When I was manager of the Cubs from 2003 to 2006 Elvin was often in Chicago and he'd come out to Wrigley Field and sit in the dugout during batting practice and take in the scene.

Later Elvin called me up and asked me if I'd like to be a presenter with him at the 2007 Blues Music Awards down in Memphis, Tennessee. Did I want to be a presenter? Of course I did. That was one of the best times I ever had, like seeing thirty concerts in two days and meeting people right and left. Charlie Musselwhite, who I'd met at John Lee's house, was a big winner, snagging Song of the Year with "Church Is Out," and Traditional Blues Album of the Year and Album of the Year with *Delta Hardware.* Elvin and I had all kinds of fun and the next day we went fishing down in Mississippi at Morgan Freeman's place. We were driving down the road and they told me that was the spot where Robert Johnson made his deal with the devil. I could feel the spiritual power of the crossroads, just like Eric Clapton sang about.

Elvin and I share another passion: gardening. He

gives me seeds or starts and that usually turns into some of the best stuff I grow in my garden out back of my house near Sacramento. A lot of those seeds he gets from Taj Mahal, and I've always admired Taj. Elvin says Taj has the best seeds in the world. Elvin travels the world playing music, and wherever he goes he keeps his eye out for seeds he wants to bring home. "I start all stuff with seed," he says. "I'm kind of a maniac about it." He especially likes going to Japan for that reason. "This Japanese seed company has created a hybrid between kale and collard greens," he told me. "I've never really liked the taste of kale, too bitter and too tough, but this is sweet and tender like collard greens." He's right about that.

One of my favorite places to go at home is the wall of my living room, where I've got a little collection of signed guitars given to me by my friends, starting with John Lee and Elvin. I've got one from B.B. King that he signed for me, and Carlos Santana and Buddy Guy, too. The one guitar missing from my collection is Eric Clapton's. One of my friends was going to arrange for me to get a guitar from Clapton, and Clapton was open to the idea, but he said I'd have to come to England to pick it up. That's a long way to fly. But I'm working on it. By the time you read this book, maybe I'll have made it over there and picked that up. All of those guitarists have given me so much pleasure over the years, so much enjoyment, that I can sit there near my collection of guitars and just groove on the good vibe.

My wall is an inspiration to me, but it's not a museum. Music is alive. It's a force that keeps you moving into the present and into the future. You can't freeze-frame it. While I was working on this last chapter, I went to a ZZ Top concert. You know, the guys originally out of Houston, with the long beards who rock hard but tap their blues roots with style. I'm not one for going to the movie theater, but I still love going to concerts, because you never quite know what you're going to see. I first caught ZZ Top back at the Cow Palace in San Francisco, where they used to have rodeos and things like that. We went backstage afterward and met the guys. I remember talking to the shorter one, whose name is also Dusty. So years later I see them again and you know what? They were just as good, maybe better.

I can time-travel through music. I might be working in the yard, but when I hear a certain cut, it gives me the feeling I've been transported to another place and time. For example, if I happen to hear

"Memphis in June" or another track from Brother Jack McDuff's album *Down Home Style*, it'll take me back to my years in Georgia when a record company executive named Fred Ware used to hook Orlando and me up with promo albums from Blue Note and Stax Records, which was where you found a lot of the best music back then. Even after the Braves traded Orlando to the A's in June 1972 for Denny McLain, Fred would take care of me and I ended up with hundreds of these promo albums. I found out later they were the best ones to have, because they were actually higher in quality. I was never into eight-track tape. I bypassed that whole thing. Starting around 1970, I would make my own cassettes, pulling tracks from those promo albums, and I did that all through the '70s. So sometimes when I hear a cut that was on one of those cassettes, that brings it all back like I'm hearing this music for the first time.

I love reggae, as I told you way back at the start of Chapter 1, and I especially love Bob Marley. He's right up there for me with Jimi Hendrix as one of my two all-time favorites. What is it about the great ones? A song like "Jammin'" or "Concrete Jungle" comes on, I hear that and it's like I tune into a whole

universe of Bob Marley. I mention those two songs
at random, but they're ones I like and they give you
the range of the man, from good-time, feel-good party
music to serious social commentary, sung soulful-
ly. I know a lot of people just tune out the words,
but even if you try, you can't ignore the power of an
opening like "No sun will shine in my day today ...
the high yellow moon won't come out to play," or the
words that come later: "No chains around my feet/
But I'm not free, oh-oooh!/ I know I am bound here
in captivity ... I've never known happiness."

Over the years I caught a lot of music at Freeborn
Hall in Davis, which for years after it opened in 1961
was the main place on the University of California
at Davis campus to see music. It was small and in-
timate, with a capacity of less than 2,000 people,
and I was lucky enough to see Bob Marley there on
December 1, 1979, barely a year and a half before he
died of a rare form of skin cancer. I'd heard he had
cancer of the toe and the way he was dancing and
grooving up on stage at Freeborn Hall, it made me
wonder if the reports were true. (I know that Rasta
doesn't believe in radiation or amputation, and when
I found out I had cancer in 2001, that kind of put me
in a quandary, because I had a young son I wanted

to watch grow up and so much to live for. Bob Marley didn't do radiation and that possibly led to his death. I chose a radical operation on my prostate, rather than radiation, and here I am today.) I've got Bob Marley painted on my motorcycle, that's how much he means to me. That night in Davis, he played "Concrete Jungle" and "Exodus" — you know, "We know where we're going; we know where we're from; we're leaving Babylon, we're going to the father-land" — and for the encore had us all going with "Get Up, Stand Up." No one ever needed to tell me get up and stand up for my rights. No one ever needed to urge me "don't give up the fight!" But sometimes it's good hearing it anyway. Ever since that concert, I don't think more than a couple of days pass with-out me listening to some Bob Marley.

All through my life, at every stage of the way, I've always had a theme song. It's good to have a theme song. You should have one, too. Like the 1979 Pittsburgh Pirates with "We Are Family" by Sister Sledge — now *that* was a theme song. For me back in high school, my theme song was "I'll Be There" by the Four Tops. I couldn't start a game until I listened to it one more time to get me ready to go. Dennis and I would be sitting in the car just before a game and

I knew I had to get out there, but I had to hear "I'll Be There" before I could go play. By the time I was with the Dodgers, I'd be choosing the theme song for the team. One year I chose "She's a Bad Mama Jama (She's Built, She's Stacked)," sung by Carl Carlton, which was one of the top singles in the country in '82. Carl Carlton himself came down to the clubhouse at Dodger Stadium because he heard we were using his hit for our theme song. The best theme songs are the ones you all know by heart, like "Super Freak," by Rick James — we'd all sing along to that one when I was with the Dodgers.

Or sometimes you pick more of a personal theme song, which you turn to not only for solace, but also for strength. That was how it was for me with "Too Long in Exile" by Van Morrison. Van the Man would be singing "Well that isolated feeling/ drives you so close up against the wall/ Till you feel like you can't go on/ You've been in the same place for too long" and I'd feel what he was feeling and it would give me strength. That and a song by Baby Cham — "Every time you knock me down I get stronger and stronger" — were very important to me when I was managing in Cincinnati, going through some tough times. Nowadays, doing all I'm doing away from baseball, from making wine to launching an energy business, I think I need a theme song that's about what Dylan called keep on keepin' on, like "Picture Me Rollin'" from 2pac: "Can you see me now? ... Move to the side a little bit so you can get a clear picture/ can you see it? Hahaha/ Picture me rollin.'"

Music keeps me young, and that's thanks also to my daughter, Natosha, and my son, Darren. They turn me on to music I might not know about. They keep me hip. Tosh turned me on to New Kids on the Block, New Addition, Salt-N-Pepa and Kid 'n Play, and I turned her on to Bob Marley, Phil Collins, Paul Simon, Howlin' Wolf, B.B. King, ZZ Top and Miles Davis and many, many more. Music has always been something we had in common. When Tosh's mother and I got divorced, she was only eight years old and after that during her summer visitations she was my roommate and I'd take her with me everywhere I went when I had the chance, up until she turned fourteen, when she came to live with me full time. We'd go to get something to eat and I'd make a point of picking a place where there would be live music. She says she can't even remember all the music she knows because of me, but it happens to her all the time that music comes on the radio that she recognizes and someone asks her how she knows it. She says, "My dad." She makes fun of me for buying a lot of CDs and always bringing them home to listen to every track at least once, but really, she's the same way most of the time. She likes all kinds of music and her first impulse is always to give something new a chance to see if she might be into it.

I go to concerts I might not otherwise go to, just so I can take my son or daughter. I took Darren and my nephew to see 50 Cent, Lil John and E-40, and I took Darren and Melissa to see Snoop Dogg. One of my favorite places is the Rock and Roll Hall of Fame in Cleveland. I took Darren and Melissa there and as we walked around, I sang along to the songs we heard, and Darren was like, "Dang, Dad, you know every song from every era!" That's the truth. It didn't matter who sang it, because the Rock and Roll Hall of Fame isn't just rock and roll. I remember back in my years with the Cubs, Buddy Guy would come see me at Wrigley Field and I'd hang out at Buddy's blues club in Chicago. He'd break out the moonshine up in the back for us some nights. I'd bring along my coaches, like Dick Pole and Wendell Kim, and I even took Darren down there. He was digging it. Buddy would walk around the room playing his guitar and you could reach in and pick his guitar as he played and hear that sound blasting out of the speakers. Darren got to do that one time and he loved it. That made him feel good and it made me feel good, knowing I was passing on music to my son and my daughter the way my daddy had passed it on to me. My dad taught me young: *If you've got the lead in life, keep the lead.* What I see now, looking back on my life and how important music has always been to me, is this: It was music that gave me the lead in life. I tell Natosha and Darren: *If you've got the lead, keep the lead.* I think it was through music that I gave my kids a lead in life.

About
the Author

J ohnnie B. Baker Jr., known since youth as Dusty, was born in Riverside, California, and went to high school at Del Campo High near Sacramento. He was drafted by the Atlanta Braves in the June 1967 amateur draft and went on to a nineteen-year Major League Baseball career, finishing with career marks of 242 home runs, 1,013 RBIs and a .278 batting average. During his ten seasons managing the San Francisco Giants starting in 1993, he was a three-time Manager of the Year and took the team to the 2002 World Series. He also managed the Chicago Cubs and Cincinnati Reds. He lives near Sacramento with his wife, Melissa, and son, Darren, and has his own energy company, Baker Energy Team. This is his first book.

About the Series

Dusty Baker's memoir of his early life, built around his mind-blowing experience of attending the 1967 Monterey Pop Festival, kicks off Wellstone Books' "Music That Changed My Life" series of books, small volumes (with cover illustrations by Mark Ulriksen) that might prompt you to lean into your love of music. They're quick reads, full of honest emotion, and if you have even half as much fun reading them as we do publishing them, we'll be happy. Wellstone Books publishes personal writing that is not afraid to inspire, and what inspires more than a deep connection to music? Coming volumes in the series include *Shop Around: Falling for Motown, Growing Up in a Sinatra Household*, by award-winning author and *San Francisco Chronicle* columnist Bruce Jenkins, and former *New York Times* columnist George Vecsey's memoir of discovering opera at an early age. We're looking for previously published authors interested in writing "Music That Changed My Life" volumes for us on Chrissie Hynde and the Clash. Query Publisher Steve Kettmann if you're potentially interested, at steve@wellstoneredwoods.org

WELLSTONE CENTER
IN THE REDWOODS

The Wellstone Center in the Redwoods, a writer's retreat in Northern California, publishes books under its Wellstone Books imprint and offers weeklong writing residencies, monthlong writing fellowships and occasional weekend writing workshops; we also host regular Author Talk events. Founded by Sarah Ringler and Steve Kettmann, WCR has been hailed in the *San Jose Mercury News* as a beautiful, inspiring environment that is "kind of like heaven" for writers, and featured in *San Francisco Magazine's* "Best of the Bay" issue. Visit our website at www.wellstoneredwoods.org for all the latest on our programs, and email at us to apply or with questions — info@wellstoneredwoods.org.

Dusty Baker will be donating the proceeds of *Kiss the Sky* to help fund our programs for young writers, in particular the "Find Your Voice" weekend writing workshop for eighteen-to-twenty-one-year-olds, and also to the Bilingual Christian Center in Sacramento.

Special Thanks

*From Sarah and Steve and everyone at the Wellstone
Center, we'd like to thank Dusty Baker for all the time he
put into telling his amazing story for us. We went into the
project thinking he was a remarkable man, and the story
that unfolds in these pages brings that impression home
all the more. Thanks also to Pete Danko, Alvaro Villanueva
and Mark Ulriksen — all of them, the best of the best —
and thanks to the friends and family members
of Dusty's who helped out with the project.*